The Shadows of Darkness: Then Came the Light

Dionne Williams Voss

Cover Photo by Marvelous Images Photography
013120

DEDICATION

To my late father for never giving up on me whenever I made mistakes and sticking with me from the very beginning until the end. To my mother for finding solace in the Lord, praying consistently and encouraging my spiritual growth.

To my husband and King, Damon, for your commitment in remaining by my side through the many storms. To my children and earthly angels, Chris, Quincey, Tori, DiMaggio and Mikel for your loving spirits and for providing me with the family lifestyle I've always desired to have. To my sister Tammy, who never allowed me to quit. I love you all so much!

This book is also dedicated to all of the helpless little children and adolescents who are struggling to find the light in the midst of the darkness.

Contents

ACKNOWLEDGMENTS

First and foremost, I thank my Heavenly Father for His amazing grace and unconditional love.

To my family and friends who encouraged and supported me along the way. A special thanks to Sharon, Sonya and Yvette for remaining by my side and creating happy times that numbed so much of the embedded pain that lied within.

To my editor and cousin, Dana; I thank you for patiently and diligently waiting so many years for me to finally develop the courage to share my story.

To our long-time family friend and photographer, Marvin L. Kelly Jr. of Marvelous Images Photography for capturing the moment through your talented photography of the inner pain that once consumed me.

To my oldest son, Chris for inspiring me with your powerful words and blessing me to clearly see that my struggles represented my 'Fight in the ring of life'. To Quincey for the tireless hours you spent working on designing and perfecting my book cover.

And last, but certainly not least, to Felicia M. for pushing me beyond my fears to share my story. I needed to hear your words of wisdom and you delivered them right on time! Thank you and much love to all of you.

Part 1

The Shadows of Darkness...

1

Baby Angel

"I was going to abort you, but Aunt Summer talked me into keeping you. She said you might make me happy someday."

This was one story of many that momma frequently shared with me as a child. Momma also explained to me that I was a product of a "One-night stand". His name was Dale and he was the neighbor and close friend of my Aunt Summer and Uncle Ced. Dale was a married man with five daughters. There'd been trouble in the marriage so his wife left him, taking their kids with her back to their home state of Texas.

It was during that time of Dale's separation from his wife that I was conceived. Momma told me she and Dale had been drinking that night and for whatever reason, at some point Dale had told momma that he was "Sterile".

Yes, well, long about the time momma learned that she was pregnant, Dale's wife came back with the kids in order to reclaim her marriage. Dale happily obliged and momma kept my growing existence a secret from many, until she began to show.

My life was just beginning from within my mother's womb and the only support and comfort momma received was provided by her only sister out of five children. She struggled to decide what would be the best decision. She was already a single parent, having had my sister Shereese six years prior. The thought of bringing another child into the mix was almost too much to consider. But after Aunt Summer convinced momma to keep me, momma spent the remainder of her pregnancy preparing for my arrival, while wondering how she would survive with two children as a single mother.

Based on the story momma shared with me, she developed a strong friendship with a man named Jace. When momma shared her story about the predicament she was in, Jace stated, "No child should be born without a father in their life". It was at that point that Jace stepped up by asking for permission to adopt me so he could become my father.

Momma agreed to allow Jace to legally adopt me and Jace vowed to take care of our family for as long as he could. Jace was a very loving and caring man and the agreement made between them would give me the benefit of having both a mother and father in my life.

Well, the big day of my birth arrived and my father, Jace had everything arranged for my mother, from health insurance to housing. Momma allowed my father to name me after one of his favorite American Pop and R&B singers, Dionne Warwick.

My father was an extremely prideful man who took life very seriously and made it a point to live life to the fullest. He was very unique in his ways, with a great sense of humor by nature. My father had a distinguished way about him and truly valued family.

What I loved about my father the most was his confidence and the tough spirit he often displayed in standing his ground by speaking up when things weren't operating in a way that he expected. He most certainly was no pushover and in fact, could be very intimidating towards others at times. He had learned to have things his way and as a child, I had to learn to adapt. He wasn't extremely strict, but still modeled somewhat of a strict parenting spirit. My father had a strong passion for life with a strong desire to help others at whatever cost and proved to be a man of his word. For as long as my mother allowed, he kept his word by providing for our family, whether it be housing, purchasing our groceries, or just meeting our basic mental and emotional needs.

Being a true man of his word, my father was consistent in picking me up early on Saturdays for us to spend the weekends together. He would take me out to eat and we'd spend the day visiting our relatives on his side of the family.

We were a close-knit family but mom struggled with being dependent on Jace. She really had a hard time and shortly into my childhood she parted ways with Jace. My father really tried to support my mother but momma wanted to do things for herself. My father agreed to give her the space she desired, but under the condition that he be allowed to remain involved in my life.

Over time, the relationship between my parents became even more strained and my father stopped coming to pick me up. Around this same time my mother started telling me that I didn't belong to Jace or his side of the family. She consistently reminded me that Jace was my "Adoptive" father. She also forbade me from call or refer to Jace as "Dad". Momma's constant reminders and the strain between my parents caused me to feel completely out of place with my father's side of the family. As the years progressed, the distance continued to expand.

I was living a life that caused me to feel entangled in the web of differences between my parents and over time, it eventually took its toll on me. I was faced with the most challenging time of my life in learning to find myself. I had to learn to figure out who I was as an individual, based on values and morals that I would have to develop on my own.

I had to learn to face and defeat many of the obstacles that were placed in my path and also learn how to pave a future that would make better sense to me in creating a sense of complete wholeness. But I first had to learn to understand the history of not only my life, but my mother's life, as well. A life that would be viewed as **A Mother's Sacrifice**

2

A Mother's Sacrifice

Momma could have repeated the cycle of abandoning us as children just like her mother had done with momma and her four siblings, but she didn't. Instead, she chose to accept the responsibility of motherhood through all of the hurt and pain she endured raising us as a single parent. Momma was a tough woman, both inside and out and fought for the things she was passionate about. Many of those fights were physical and occurred primarily with the men momma allowed in her life.

As a little girl, I was extremely kind-spirited and unfortunately, my kindness angered my mother whenever she thought I was being too soft towards others. She began to physically punish me for not standing up for myself.

By the time I reached my preschool years, physical punishment had become the only form of discipline I experienced. I had grown accustomed to receiving slaps in the face, not only figures of authority, but also by my peers.

Momma started the trend when I was in preschool. I had innocently shared with her that I had a boyfriend. Of course, I told her my news out of pure happiness, but after sharing what I thought would be an exciting story, I soon realized that I should've kept my story to myself.

Just prior to my mother arriving to pick me up, I happened to be sitting next to another little preschooler named Mark. While sitting next to one another, Mark reached down, gently grabbed my hand and our little hands remained interlocked right up until it was time for me to leave. Mark's spirit seemed so gentle, warm and kind and created a sense of peace within me.

I wanted to make certain my mother saw me holding hands with this sweet fella', so when I noticed momma walking through the door I made sure to stand up, while still holding onto Mark's little hand. I was so proud to show I had a boyfriend and desired so badly for her to see our sweet little innocent hands clasped together.

Well, it turned out that momma didn't even notice. Momma motioned for me to come to her so she could get me into my coat and hat. Without a word, we exited the preschool building and went on our way. Momma didn't have a car at the time, so we had to walk to the bus stop. While we were waiting, I decided to tell momma the great news about my boyfriend since she hadn't noticed.

"Guess what momma? I have a boyfriend and we were holding hands today".

Within moments of relaying the news about my new boyfriend, momma turned towards me, looked down at me, then slapped me out of what felt like pure anger. She sternly expressed her disapproval of me having a boyfriend. She told me I was not allowed to have a boyfriend and that she didn't want to hear anything further about him.

The excitement of me having a boyfriend faded quickly and I knew at that point that I'd never again feel comfortable in sharing another story with my mother about a boy.

I didn't want to experience being slapped again by my mother, so I abided by her instruction and from that day moving forward, remained distant from the boys at my daycare. I know momma was doing her best to keep me steered in the right direction without becoming distracted by boys at such a young age and unfortunately, I had to learn the hard way. I managed to avoid encountering a slap in the face by my mother during those early years, but this corporal means of discipline and treatment seemed to manifest its way back into my life by other trusted authority figures who played a role during my early stages of development.

During my pre-kindergarten year, I was sitting at a table with my classmates. We were all coloring, using crayons from a box the teacher had placed in the middle of the table. A boy named Randy, who was sitting directly across from me took a strong hold to a crayon I had selected from the crayon box. Randy was set on using the crayon I had picked up and decided that he was going to snatch it from my hand. I gripped the crayon tightly, determined that I would win the battle.

Randy and I tugged back and forth on the crayon until it broke. At that point our teacher, Ms. Brenda looked over in our direction with a very angry expression. She walked over to our table, turned towards me and slapped me across my little face with her huge hand.

There was complete silence as the rest of my classmates and teacher's assistants stared at us. I was so hurt and humiliated. I wanted to hide and not be seen but unfortunately, I had no way of escaping. Instead I buried my head in my little hands, then gently placed my head on the table and cried.

Ms. Brenda's focus was solely on me and she never touched, scolded or said anything to Randy for his actions involving the broken crayon. All I could think of at the time was, "Why me?"

When momma arrived to pick me up that day she noticed the red bruising on my face. As we walked to the bus stop she questioned me about what had happened. After I explained the situation to her she became very upset and by the next morning, had called a meeting with Ms. Brenda and her assistants to discuss the matter.

My mother made it very clear to my teachers that they were not to place their hands on me for any reason. Ms. Brenda cried as she apologized to my mother. She explained that she'd been under a high degree of stress after having just learned that her son was sentenced to prison.

My mother heard Ms. Brenda's reasoning, but sure didn't allow Ms. Brenda to use her excuse as a form of justification for her actions in slapping me. Momma made sure that Ms. Brenda understood her concerns as a parent. Ms. Brenda understood quite well, because I never encountered another issue with any of my pre-kindergarten teachers beyond that point.

It wasn't until I reached the second grade at a new K – 8 school that I encountered another slap in my face. I was excited for the change of my new school and also very excited to be closer to my sister Shereese, who attended the same school.

It was my first day of second grade and Shereese happened to run into one of her classmates named Gene, who had a little sister assigned to the same classroom as I had been assigned to. Gene introduced me to his sister, Erita and asked her if she could hang out with me for the day to help me become acquainted with other schoolmates. Erita gladly accepted and started off very sweet, but by lunch time Erita's attitude had changed. She became bossy and started bullying me around on the playground. During our lunch recess, Erita instructed me to follow her around as she gathered a few girls from our class together. Once we were all gathered in a group, Erita instructed all of us to sit down on the ground in a circle. Erita then told us that we were in her club and would do exactly what she instructed us to do.

As Erita proceeded to speak, she stated in an authoritative manner that if we did not do what she told us to do, "This will happen", and that is when she turned towards me, raised her hand and wham… slapped me hard in my face. She was demonstrating that she meant business, while also attempting to instill fear in all of the girls in the club. It worked. The girls in our group froze and stared at me with surprised expressions on their faces. Not only had I been blindsided, but every girl involuntarily nominated to participate in the club had been blindsided, as well.

All I could think of was the fact that it had happened again. I had endured yet another instance of complete humiliation. For whatever reason, I'd become Erita's target for harsh treatment. I just couldn't understand why I had to deal with such cruel treatment from others who felt compelled to inflict pain upon me. Was I too nice? Was I weak? I made up my mind that I would not keep this from my mother and couldn't wait to get home to talk to her and share the story of how badly I was treated by this mean girl at my new school. I just knew momma would be able to help me and I had complete trust and faith in her ability to provide me with the best advice and guidance in facing Erita the next day, so when I made it home, I immediately approached momma to tell her all about my first day. "Mom, what would you do if someone slapped you?" was how I worded the question and it was at that moment, I realized that my approach in turning to my mother for support was a failed one because all hell broke loose. Momma angrily responded with, "Did you let someone else hit you, Dionne?"

It was one of the moments that my mother flew off of the handle and I was caught like a deer in the headlights. I soon realized that my idea in approaching momma was not a good idea and knew I was in trouble.

Momma didn't allow me much of an opportunity to explain the situation. The only thing she heard was "Yes", *I had allowed someone to hit me*. Momma instructed me to get the belt, which were the words I despised hearing during my young years. I could not understand what I had done wrong, but knew I was in big trouble.

I obeyed momma and got the belt as she had instructed me to do. I was scared and began to cry. Momma was yelling at me as she started whipping me with the belt. As I screamed in fear of being whipped, I laid down, rolling from side to side to avoid being hit.

"You will learn to stick up for yourself and not allow others to keep hurting you, Dionne! Every time you allow someone to hurt you, I am going to spank you!"

The whipping by momma seemed to last forever. A whipping that would later contribute to me becoming more deeply involvement in a very cruel and violent world. I had to figure out a way to protect myself from the evil doings of others. I would have to learn how to stick up for myself because there sure wasn't anyone else who was going to do it for me. My sole mission was to survive and I was willing to do whatever was necessary to prevent others from hurting me. I also had to do what was necessary to keep momma from ever spanking me again. I refused to give momma another reason to spank me. I knew that in order to survive, I had to learn to release all fear and care I had for others by learning to stick up for myself.

Momma's way of handling what she perceived as a weakness in me was to spend a lot of time teaching me how to physically fight. That was her way of toughening up my kind-hearted spirit. She wanted me to learn how to protect myself.

I can still visualize momma standing in our living room with her fists balled up, demonstrating her fighting techniques. She'd tell me to imitate her actions. Momma's training came at the right time because I soon learned that I was preparing for the time when **Darkness Falls**.

3

Darkness Falls

Momma met Hades when I was five years old. I noticed right away that Hades wasn't a very nice man, but I still modeled respect towards him because I knew his presence in our home made momma happy. But as time progressed, so did Hades' violence towards my mother. He started off somewhat charming and intriguing; however, it wasn't long before we realized he was an angry beast and ticking time bomb. Even at that young age I recognized the lack of love and compassion this angry beast had for my mother. His charming demeanor deteriorated quickly into years of beatings my mother would have to endure. At seven years old I vowed to attempt in every way to save my mother from this extremely evil man.

There was one night that he came to our home, pounding on the front door while yelling to be let in. My mother told us not to let him in, so we sat and listened to the brutal sounding bangs he made at the door. When he realized my mother was not going to open the door he began to circle our home, walking from the front door to the back, repeatedly banging on them in a hellish manner as if he was attempting to break them down. All the while, he was yelling that momma would never leave him.

My mother finally gave in and unlocked the door, allowing the beast to enter and by then, he was furious. As soon as he came inside we realized he had reached his peak of anger. He stormed through the house, heading straight for my mother. His plan? To beat her as he'd become accustomed to doing.

My mother had been ironing our clothes earlier that day and had left the iron cooling on the board in the kitchen. Hades picked up the iron and charged towards my mother.

I remember my first thought being, "This mean man is not going to hurt my mother!" I was going to do whatever was necessary to stop that from happening.

I ran towards him from behind and leapt up onto his back, trying my hardest to attack him with every little bit of strength I had in my seven-year-old body. I quickly realized that my attempt to save my mother was nothing in comparison to the rage he was feeling. He seemed to have an absence of care for anyone in the home and it really didn't matter that I was a young child.

He easily pushed me off, throwing me across the kitchen floor with severe force. It was then that I realized I would not be able to protect my mother as I had so desired. I fell hard onto the floor, sliding up against the wall of our kitchen. It was at that time that I realized there was nothing I could do to protect my mother and therefore, allowed him to have his way, while hearing the yelling, screaming and fighting.

My quiet little atmosphere had become so noisy and violent. This man entered our home with the intention of hurting my protector and I could not do a damn thing about it. I sat in fear, crying and wondering how someone could be so angry and mean. As a child I was helpless. This would be a behavior I'd have to accept from this extremely angry man.

His rages grew even worse after my mother became pregnant with his child, leaving me to feel completely helpless and hopeless for myself and my mother. My sister escaped his wrath. Momma speculated that Hades feared Shareese's father, which left me and my mother to bear the brunt of his physical attacks.

It wasn't long before he started inflicting wounds so severe to momma's body that she'd become unrecognizable. Momma believed that Hades loved her and continued to give him chances to change. Unfortunately, Hades did not change. He just grew bolder with his abuse, even at times making sexual advances towards me right in front of momma. She'd yell at him to stop and Hades would laugh it off.

After my mother delivered my brother Jeris, there was a night she attempted to regain her freedom. She went to hang out with a close friend who frequently hosted social gatherings at his home. Prior to leaving, momma provided us with her usual instructions of not answering the door, or allowing anyone into our home while she was away. Again, it was one of those evenings that Hades arrived, pounding on the door as he demanded for us to tell him where momma was. He had noticed momma's car was not parked out front in her usual parking spot. As specifically instructed by momma, my sister and I did not respond.

While momma was out, she had no idea Hades was driving through the neighborhood in his truck looking for her. He was familiar with the places she frequently visited and was able to find her easily. We had no idea what was going on until Hades called to tell us the frightening truth.

I remember hearing our phone ring in the middle of the night and getting out of bed. I heard my sister asking Hades what he had done to our mother before demanding that he put momma on the phone. Shereese made several attempts to communicate with momma but seemed to struggle with understanding momma's words. That is when Shereese demanded to speak with Hades again. I was scared when I heard Shereese ask, "What would you do if I did that to your mother?" Eventually, the call ended and I was left wondering what had happened to momma.

The next morning, Hades drove up in his truck. My sister and I ran outside. I remember seeing dried drops of blood spattered all on the inside of the passenger side window. The truck door opened and my mother got out, her face was completely disfigured. She'd been beaten so badly that we could barely identify her. When she tried to speak, her words were mushy and indistinct. I will never forget how she looked for the rest of my life

We later learned that when Hades found out where our mother was after locating her car, he used his truck to ram her car onto her friend's lawn. The commotion of course caused momma and her friends step outside of her friend's house and that is when he forced her to get in his truck, beating her the entire time it took for him to drive back to his apartment.

I recall sitting on the couch after we got my mother into the house. I sat next to her, staring at her disfigured face, while silently questioning her understanding of what true love was. I vividly recall thinking, "This can't be love!"

I stared at her, not really knowing what to say, or how to respond. As a young child, it is so hard to process something of that nature and even more difficult to express yourself.

I was still trying to figure out why my mother had allowed this crazy man into our lives. I'm sure she'd grown to become afraid of him and what he was capable of doing. At that point in my mother's life, I believe she felt as though she had no way out of this hell she'd found herself in. By then, she had also delivered Hades' child and was bonded to this unhealthy man for life.

In the midst of all of the turmoil and abuse, momma had lost her city job. She allowed Hades to convince her to withdraw us from the expensive private schools we'd been attending and we all moved into Hades' home. Momma's decision to move in with Hades eventually led to a time I would endure one of the worst beatings of my young life.

I had returned home from school and was preparing to complete my homework as my mother had always instructed me to do. Hades came in, looked at me with his evil eyes, demanding I stop what I was doing to go polish his boots. In response to his demand, I replied with, "My momma told me to finish my homework," and he firmly stated, "I told you to polish my damn boots!"

Hades felt I had disrespected him by talking back, so as a consequence for speaking up and not obeying this evil man, he instructed me to pull a chair out from the kitchen into the living room.

I had no idea what this man had planned to do, but I obeyed and got the chair. Hades wore a huge leather belt with his name engraved in large letters on the leather strap of his belt. As I pulled the chair into the room, he began to remove his belt from the belt loops of his jeans. He told me to bend over the chair, then began to beat me with the belt. I held on to the chair, sobbing and begging for relief, all while trying to understand what I had done wrong. I was whipped until my mother returned home from work. She barged in, yelling at him and asking me what had happened. After I explained what had happened, she returned to yelling at him about how she expected me to prioritize my homework and he turned towards her and began beating her with the same belt. He beat her as she screamed and cried, until she was cowering in the corner of the room. My mother couldn't save me and so I ended up sitting on the floor in a backroom, polishing this mean man's boots with tears streaming down my face.

There were a couple more violent episodes before my mother finally had enough of this crazy man and called it quits. Momma had opened the doors to a trap that was difficult to escape from, but she managed to find a way out, accepting the fact that her relationship with Hades had failed. One morning after Hades left for work, momma instructed us to pack up as many of our personal belongings as we possibly could and we left for good. The sad part in us having to escape so suddenly was the fact that we had to leave my pet goldfish behind, which surprisingly survived until momma was able to return to pick him up many weeks later.

Momma took us to a very large home where other women and their children were living, later explaining to us that we were in a safe house where we would remain until momma was able to locate housing on her own.

All of the other mothers and children were there for the same reason; to escape from their abusive partners. The safe house provided the victims of abuse with the tools to become more self-sufficient before sending them on their way to live independently in a much safer community.

There were strict conditions required of the residents at the safe house and in order to remain compliant, it was imperative for all to abide by their rules. Some of the rules required momma and the other residents to sign up and take turns completing various chores, such as cooking the meals, cleaning and attending various support groups.

The time we spent there seemed like an eternity. When Christmas season rolled around I accepted that the safe house had become our new home. We didn't see any of our outside family; just us and the families we resided with within the safe house.

Momma's decision to escape from Hades turned out to be one of the best decisions she'd ever made as a single mother of three children, because she learned to take a stance in prioritizing her children. For once, a man was no longer being placed before us. Momma learned to stand up to Hades by her actions, as if to say "No more!" and her efforts saved us from Hades ever hurting us again. Shereese remained untouched by Hades and while Jeris was young, he also escaped being harmed by Hades. It was just me and mom who were the victims of this evil man.

Through momma building up the confidence to leave Hades, she taught us the importance of reclaiming our lives, in addition to teaching us that domestic abuse would no longer be tolerated in our home.

We moved from the safe house to a large duplex owned by my grandfather in the Five Points community. Momma shared with us that it happened to be the house she'd lived in as a child.

My grandfather, who was a strict man was now our landlord and although he had the reputation of being strict, grandpa also had a heart of gold, with the best desires for his family members to succeed in life.

Our place was one of two properties in the neighborhood owned by my grandfather. The other was just two blocks away and also the location where my grandfather's two brothers and their children resided. Despite being so close in distance, we weren't very close as a family. I did manage to maintain a very special relationship with my great uncle, who was very sweet and spent a lot of time talking to me whenever I'd visit him at his apartment.

After making the decision to leave Hades, momma never returned. Hades had become history, but the emotional and mental scars that Hades left behind lasted for many years to follow and the only hope we had was leaning on the lessons of **Guardian Angels** to get us through.

4

Guardian Angels

During the years that our lives were more stable, momma spent a lot of time reading spiritual books to me with illustrations of baby angels. One of my favorite books was about an elderly married couple who were also grandparents and had reached the end-stages of their lives. They'd fallen ill and were close to dying.

During the final moment of their lives, many baby angels, in the form of cherubs flew down from the sky, gently grabbed their hands and led them back up into the clouds. The elderly couple had such peaceful and joyful looks on their faces. The cute little baby cherubs always caught my attention and comforted my soul. These were the types of angels I always imagined were watching over and protecting me when I encountered unsafe situations.

Along with the spiritual books, momma also read the comics to me from the newspapers, which she often referred to as "The funnies". She would also read articles that she thought were important.

One day, after reading the funnies momma came across an article about an attempted abduction of a child that she made a point to read to me.

The article told the story of a man who forced a little girl into a car, but the little girl was able to escape by jumping out of the car and running away. That article would later save me from being abducted.

I was seven years old at the time and momma made sure to teach me well about "Stranger danger", but unfortunately her teachings did not include being wary of possible impersonators of law enforcement. I always believed in and had a lot of respect and trust in law enforcement officers because I was taught that they were trustworthy.

It was a cold day during my second grade year, when momma received a call from our school administrator. She was informed about my illness and advised to pick up early from school. Unfortunately, it happened to be the same day momma had a job interview scheduled. I knew this interview was important. Mom had been struggling to pay the high cost tuition for me and Shereese to attend private schools.

After picking me up early from school, momma relayed to me that she had a job interview and told me I would have to remain in the car during the interview. As she pulled into the parking lot she gave me specific instructions to keep all of the doors locked and to not open them for any strangers. She got out of the car and I locked the doors as instructed. I sat there waiting patiently for momma to return.

I was sitting in the car with my big winter coat on and my school books and mittens stacked on top of my lap, I noticed a white car slowly pull up along the passenger's side of our vehicle. Back then, it was not uncommon, or an unlawful act for parents to leave their children inside of the car for any set amount of time, but I'm certain many parents were aware of the risks involved, as my own mother was.

After pulling up, I noticed the car was still running. I glanced over and saw a Black man with an afro staring right at me. He gestured for me to roll down the window. I ignored his gestures until he held up what appeared to be a law enforcement badge. This man seemed to have no intention of leaving until he spoke with me. Since he had flashed his badge, I assumed he was a trustworthy police officer. I rolled down my window to see what he wanted and that is when he asked me who I was waiting for.

It was my first strike in disobeying momma's instruction by talking to a stranger. I responded by telling him that momma was meeting with someone in the building behind us and would be back soon. He made mention of it being a cold day and asked me if I was cold. I told him I was fine. He said he had his heat on while his car was running since it was cold and made an offer for me to sit in his car with him until momma returned. I told him that momma instructed me not to leave the car and he said I'd be fine. He promised that he would remain parked in the spot until momma returned. I felt the need to model respect to this man who appeared to be an officer since he had a badge and seemed nice, so I accepted his offer. I gathered my belongings and got into his car.

A few minutes later after getting in, the man shifted his running car in reverse and started backing away from the parking spot. I started panicking as I looked from side to side, wondering why this man was not keeping his word and instead, taking me away. I remember feeling scared, as I started to cry but then suddenly I remembered the article about the little girl who had escaped the attempted abduction.

I immediately grabbed the door handle, opened the door while the car was still moving and jumped out. My books and gloves were scattered all over the ground of the parking lot as I rolled out of the car. As quickly as I could, I jumped up and ran away. I was crying and screaming for someone to help me. I had really trusted this man's word and now he had betrayed me.

As I was running, I noticed a lady walking towards me and ran right into her arms. I wrapped my little arms around her waist, gripping so tightly that she could barely move. I frantically begged for her to help me. I told her that a man tried to drive away with me in his car. The lady embraced me and told me to calm down. She began to question me and I explained that momma was at a job interview inside of the building. Within minutes I was reunited with my mother and of course she was extremely upset with me for disobeying her instructions and getting into a car with a stranger.

Later, when momma and I talked about that scary incident, she told me that the man had remained at the site after I jumped out of his car. He kept claiming to be an undercover detective and explained that his reason for driving off with me was to drop me off at Child Protective Services since I was left alone in the car.

Momma was never able to verify his true identity. It was also unusual that after the incident, momma was never contacted and questioned about the matter by any other individual or agency. Momma told me that she did not believe his story and was convinced that he was impersonating the role of an undercover detective.

As the years progressed, I crossed paths with that same man, wandering up and down the escalators alone, in a downtown retail store. I was hanging out with my friends at the time and freaked out when I saw him. I turned to head in the opposite direction in an effort to hide from him, doing my best to avoid being seen or making eye contact with him. Since he was by himself, I assumed he was looking for underage and unsupervised children to pick up.

I realized it was a huge mistake in disobeying momma's instructions and nearly paid the price for my actions. I believe that if momma had not taken the time to share that

The Shadows of Darkness: Then Came the Light

article with me about the little girl jumping out of the car to escape from being abducted, I would not have thought to jump out of the moving car I was in. I am also grateful that the automobiles made during that era in time did not include automatic and childproof locks as they do today, or things would have turned out quite different for me. While I will never know where I could have ended up, or even who I could have ended up with, I will always believe in my heart and soul that guardian angels were watching over me, even during times I experienced **Violations** by **Authority** figures in my life.

27

5

Violation of Authority

By the time I reached my preschool years, physical punishment had become my mother's chosen form of discipline for me. This form of corporal correction seemed to manifest its way into other areas of my life by other trusted authority figures who played a role during my early stages of development.

It was proving difficult for me to find anyone of authority I could trust. I learned I had to be wary of everyone, even members of my family.

My mother's only sister and mother figure had passed, so her stepsister was pretty much all my mother had in terms of a supportive female in her life. Momma's relationship with her stepsister wasn't always the best. In fact, I don't believe there was any good in their relationship. I remember momma sharing sad stories about how unfairly she and her older sister had been treated by their stepmother and how their stepmother had always shown favoritism towards her own daughter over my mother and her older sister. At this point in momma's life though, she didn't have anyone else to turn to, so she periodically had to rely on her stepsister to babysit me and my sister, whenever necessary.

The ill-feelings between momma and her stepsister seemed to trickle down and affect the relationship Shereese and I had with our step-cousins. My step-aunt had two daughters who were near our age and both were complete bullies. They definitely seemed to have no love or genuine concern for us. Therefore, none of the visits were pleasant.

The four of us would be sent out to the backyard to play and the actions of my step-cousins were far from playful. My sister and I tried keeping our distance from them but there was nowhere to hide. As a small child, it often felt as though we were terrorized every time we visited. My sister and I both learned it was best to keep quiet.

There was a time momma dropped me off alone and this time was by far the most traumatic out of all visits I had ever experienced. I was only three years old and still remember 'til this day.

As usual, we were sent out to the backyard to play. I remember being left with the youngest of my step-cousins. My step-aunt instructed her to watch after me. I remember my step-aunt specifically telling her not to leave me alone with their dogs because they would bite me. They had two huge German Shepherds who were locked in a fenced area.

My step-cousin asked me if I wanted to feed the dogs through the fence and of course I accepted the offer. As I squatted down to feed the dogs, my step-cousin watched me with a faint smile. She gave me another handful of dog food and instructed me to continue feeding the dogs while she went back inside of the house. As soon as my step-cousin entered the house I was attacked by one of the dogs.

Instead of taking the food from my little hand, the dog went into attack mode and repeatedly bit into my arm, his big teeth deeply penetrating through my skin. I was startled by how quickly this dog's mood had changed. I stood up from my squatted position, crying out as I struggled to yank my arm out of this fierce dog's mouth. I was terrified that he would manage to bite my arm clean off.

While screaming in agony from the excruciating and intense pain as the dog maintained his grip, I urinated on myself and my body went into complete shock.

I remember clearly that my step-aunt ran out of the house into the backyard, yelling at her daughter for leaving me alone with their vicious dogs. I believe her coming outside was the only reason the dog eventually released my little arm. Beyond that, the rest of the day is a blur. I don't remember if I was taken to the doctor and I definitely don't remember my mother returning right away to get me.

Every time I see the scar from the large tooth of that vicious dog, I feel extremely grateful that I was able to overcome that horrific attack and thank God that this dog was at least locked inside of a fenced area, or the ordeal could've been much worse, even fatal. Thankfully I survived and the strength I developed afterwards assisted me in dealing with **The Chains of Bondage** that were gradually and invisibly becoming entangled around my hands and feet.

6

The Chains of Bondage

Growing up in my world, violence and anger had become a huge part of my life. I learned to adapt to it, embrace it and in many instances, I became a part of it. With so many of the struggles I had experienced without the protection I felt I deserved as a growing child, there really was nowhere for me to escape in order to seek help, so I was left in a tragic situation of trying to save myself as I searched for my own direction towards the light.

As a child, I related the most to Bill Bixby's character, Dr. Bruce Banner, in the original 1970's show, *The Incredible Hulk*. I was intrigued by how kind the character, Dr. Banner was until being pushed to the edge, where he'd then transform into the Hulk. I too would suppress my anger until it reached a boiling point of explosion. Once I was angry, that feeling would be taken to an entirely different level.

Sometimes, I really think the show, coupled with the whippings I got from momma for failing to fight back is what influenced me to let my anger loose. At my young age, I didn't have any other outlets or options in knowing how to channel my anger and therefore, had to find my own way to survive, so reaching the point of explosion seemed to be the only necessary means I had. I knew momma sure wasn't going to allow me to continue being the patient and kind hearted little girl that others could take advantage of. Forcing me to stick up for myself was momma's way of teaching me how to survive.

My first outburst of anger occurred during my fourth grade year. This was the same time momma had withdrawn me and my sister from the private school system and moved us all in with Hades. That year was very unstable for me as I ended up being transferred to three different public schools. Along with the abuse I suffered at home, I became completely overwhelmed.

The first school I enrolled in during my fourth grade year started out fairly smooth. There were many kids in the neighborhood that I became acquainted with and also played with on a daily basis. The neighborhood I lived in was quite like sharing my life with a family that I saw throughout the day. I spent a lot of time playing outdoors.

What was unfortunate was the fact that we didn't reside in the neighborhood for very long. Before I could get comfortable, momma and Hades decided to move to another home with more space, much further away. After moving into the new home, momma enrolled me in a new school. I didn't know many people and didn't have any friends, but I didn't mind. I also hadn't encountered any problems with other peers causing problems with me. Life at the new school was quite peaceful, even though my home life was not.

My favorite subject in school was reading and it was evident, as I continued to progress through reading levels. The time momma spent reading to me really paid off. I seemed to thrive so well in reading that my homeroom teacher placed me on an individual reading program. Once every other week, a huge bus called the Book Mobile traveled to our school with books for us to check out and I felt I was in heaven every time I stepped onto that mobile bus to check out new books.

Unfortunately, I never had the opportunity to fully adjust to my new school. Before I had the opportunity to get settled in, momma developed the courage to leave Hades. So once again, I was pulled out of school during my fourth grade year and enrolled in my third school. I didn't know much about the neighborhood we were residing in. I was just happy that we were living a much safer lifestyle, but soon realized my main concern would be learning to survive in the streets because trouble was on the way and coming head on, much like a railroad train moving at top speed.

With all of the trauma I had encountered within a year's time, many of my memories of what seemed like happy times began to fade away. I really wasn't sure where I belonged in the world and life just didn't seem as pleasant as it once was before momma started dating Hades and sacrificed our safety and wellbeing. We, as a family were now paying the price for it and at that time, momma was just trying to survive by simply holding on to whatever she had the ability to by that time in our lives. Our lives had changed drastically… particularly mine.

The future of my life had become much like a mystery and there was no way to determine whether I would return to living my life as the sweet little innocent girl that I was born into this world as, or the fighter that momma had spanked me to become. It was my choice to resume with being nice, or to allow the beast inside of me to emerge.

It was just a matter of time before I learned to allow myself to become a product of my environment. My life had been turned upside down and we had become caught up in a struggle of poverty. What a trap we had become entangled in and it seemed I was paying a huge price for the detours momma took in her mission to find love and happiness. Life was good and stable for me at one point and everything seemed to be going well until I was thrown in with the wolves after transferring to my third school within one full calendar school year. That year by far, was one of the most challenging and traumatic experiences of my life.

As a result of the transition we experienced as a family in that one year's time, my grades dropped so low that I was required to attend summer school. This was the summer leading into my fifth grade year and by then my life had emerged into complete darkness. I had allowed that inner beast to emerge and had already experienced my first fight at my newest school. I was angry and no longer cared much about my life and it showed. The pain was real… very real and the only hope I seemed to have in life was my hope to survive.

I perceived my life as a bad deck of cards that had been dealt to me that I had initially accepted before realizing that I did not have to. I learned to use what skills I had to play against that hand that was dished out to me in order to survive. I refused to continue settling for the short end of the stick, but I learned that my refusal would entail taking on more risks, exhibiting more anger and engaging in many more physical fights than what I had ever imagined… all for the purpose of trying to escape the madness. I seemed to have no other choice available to me but to join the dark side of life in order to have a chance at getting out and unfortunately, I had to fall very deep into what I considered as the pit of living hell.

My first day of summer school arrived and my experience wasn't at all what I had expected. The school was nearly three miles of a distance from where I lived, so I was transported by a school bus. I just had the responsibility of walking to my home school for the school bus to transport me from that point.

When I arrived and found the classroom I was assigned to, I entered, sat down and waited for my teacher, Ms. Snide to take attendance. The room was hot and it sure didn't help that Ms. Snide wasn't friendly. It seemed that neither of us had a desire to be there and she sure didn't make it easy for me in my effort to try and connect with her, so it most certainly was no "win-win" situation. I felt as though I was doomed for the entire summer and therefore, extremely unhappy. There I was, sitting in a hot classroom learning nothing from a mean teacher, which caused my anger to reach a boiling point.

I had become fed up and one hot summer day, I responded in the most negative way towards Ms. Snide. Of course, nothing that was planned. It just occurred all of a sudden and I yelled at Ms. Snide, stormed out of the classroom and left the school building without permission. I just wanted out of that school, so I took control of the matter and left.

By that point in my life I was learning to function in complete darkness; a time when many trials and tribulations seemed to consume me, involving the physical abuse I had to endure, the homelessness we had struggled to overcome while having to live with strangers over the Christmas and New Year's holidays and the survival tactics I had to adopt in my effort to protect myself in a neighborhood and school with such cruel kids. Everything seemed to catch up with me at the same time and Ms. Snide had become a target for me to unleash every ounce of anger I had learned over the years to bottle up inside.

In my ability to reflect, I know there a lesson in everything that took place that day for me to learn from. One of the scariest and most unexplainable times in my life occurred after storming out of the school and taking my load of unhealthy baggage with me.

I had set out to walk the entire way home and as I was walking I heard the sound of crows from a distance in the trees, which wasn't unusual to hear. What was unusual was the fact that the crows were interested in me, which I realized when their loud caws intensified as I continued to stroll down the long path of trees aligned along both sides of the streets. There were several crows, each taking turns to swoop down lower and lower from the trees located on both sides. Up until that point in my life I had never encountered problems with any birds, so I was completely caught off guard by their actions.

I had traveled down this road plenty of times in my life, so I initially didn't pay any mind to any of the birds until I realized how close they were flying towards my head, almost appearing as if they were planning an attack on me. When I realized all of these crows were focused on me I started to run as fast as I could. I had no idea why these wild birds were coming after me and still, 'til this day question their actions. What I do know, is that the experience caused my anger to fade away very quickly and in turn, I became quite terrified.

I never forgot that day and always believed in my heart and soul that there was some deep spiritual meaning and lesson behind it. While I was able to get away from the wild crows without being attacked, the experience taught me about the importance of learning to control the rage that seemed to be manifesting inside of me. I felt as though I had placed myself in danger by abruptly leaving the school, accepting the fact that anything could've happened to me. That is the day I realized that evil breeds evil.

That was one of the first times in my life that I felt alone during my journey in having to try and process what I was going through in order to better understand why my anger had grown to become so out-of- control. I realized it was left up to me to figure out how to turn away from the dark road I was headed down, but at that time I had absolutely no idea how to even begin to grasp control over many of the situations I ended up in. I was just too young to deal with so many issues on my plate and most certainly lacked the skills necessary to handle matters more appropriately.

The message I took away that day involving my encounter with the crows will always remain as one that is deeply rooted with a strong spiritual meaning behind it for the journey I was traveling at the time, and one that I'll never forget. As time passed, I learned that the dark days I was experiencing were only the beginning to a very dark and bleak future that I would have to learn to escape from on my own and it was quite evident that it wouldn't be an easy task because I was entering a ring of vicious **Cycles** that seemed to be **Awakening.**

7

The Cycle Awakens

By the age of nine my life seemed to be spiraling downwards towards a point of no return and what made it even tougher was knowing that I severely lacked the tools to do what was necessary to keep myself afloat socially and academically. My support system had diminished greatly. The relationship I'd had with Jace was gone and momma had emotionally and mentally disconnected from me during her time of healing from escaping Hades' brutal abuse.

By momma's choice to shut out the world, I often felt as though we were living our lives in complete isolation. She had cut the involvement of extended family members out of my life; mostly cousins from both sides of my family who were around my age.

I had spent some time reflecting on how much my life had changed. My first few years of elementary school were spent attending parochial schools, until momma gave up her independence by giving in to Hades. By then, we'd lost everything, including momma's sense of control, basically leaving us with the only option of having to start all over.

By the end of my fourth grade year I had transferred to three different public schools as a result of all of the transitions that occurred in our lives. We moved a lot during that time which made it difficult for me when it came to developing healthy friendships with other kids my age. Until that point, making friends was never a problem for me and I sure hadn't encountered any problems with other kids desiring to engage in physical altercations with me, but that soon changed in the new community we had moved to.

The last school I had transferred to was by far, the most difficult one for me to adjust to. I was assigned to Mr. Jacks' classroom, which happened to be the most disruptive classroom of all of the fourth grade classes. After being introduced to Mr. Jacks, he asked me what reading level I was on and what book I had been reading out of at my last school and when I told him, he appeared puzzled.

When life was more stable for us, before Hades was allowed in our lives, momma made many trips to the children's library for me to check out books that I could read on my own. By then, reading had become a well-liked hobby for me that kept me content, so there was no doubt that my reading level was much higher than most of the kids in Mr. Jacks' class.

After providing Mr. Jacks with my reading level, instead of assigning me to what should have been the most appropriate group, he seemed to randomly select what turned out to be the lowest and most disruptive reading group in the classroom, full of the most disruptive boys. It was a group that I never gained the opportunity to progress from.

My "reading" days consisted of being teased, bullied and inappropriately touched by these boys. They'd do things like brushing their hands across my breasts as they passed by my desk, all the while laughing out loud as if to alert all of their class buddies that they had scored with their inappropriate touching. Leading up to that point in my life, I had no clue that kids could be so cruel.

The class I was assigned to was under the full control of the students and the experience was horrific for me. I grew to hate school with a passion and spent every single day walking in the classroom with my eyes flushed with tears. I wanted to escape and unfortunately, there was nowhere to hide, so I was forced to deal with every bit of humiliation those mean kids subjected me to.

The day I was assigned to Mr. Jacks' class was the day I stopped learning for the remainder of my fourth grade year. Mr. Jacks struggled to maintain organization and control in the classroom and eventually resigned from his position as our homeroom teacher. After Mr. Jacks resigned, the bullying grew to become so bad for me that I had no choice but to fight back as momma had taught me to do in an effort to create some sense of control for myself. After the buildup of the physical abuse that had been inflicted upon me, in addition to the teasing and bullying I encountered from my peers, I had reached a point of explosion and by then, momma couldn't even control me.

The problems I was encountering within the school began to manifest outside of the school, filtering out into the community, as well.

One of the issues I encountered in the community was when I was approached by two teenage girls who were walking down the street of the block I resided on. Two guys had come over to visit my sister, Shereese and we all walked down to a restaurant not far from our house.

We were heading back and I decided to walk about a block ahead. As I was crossing the street I noticed two older teenage girls coming down the street. Although I noticed the girls, I didn't think much of them as I proceeded to cross the street. That is when one of them yelled out, "Look at that bitch, she thinks she's cute".

The blunt statement from one of the girl's completely caught me off-guard because I was not used to being confronted like that for no reason, at least not outside of school. I had no idea who I was dealing with, but by that time I'd grown tired and weary, primarily from being picked on at school and spanked by momma for failing to stand up for myself. I had toughened up to say the least, so even though these girls were much older, I knew that if I allowed them to get the best of me without attempting to fight back, momma would tear my butt up when I got home and I sure wasn't having that.

After hearing the crude comment from one of the girls, I immediately responded with, "What? Why I gotta be a bitch? I haven't said or done anything to you!"

It was at that point that I realized that responding to the girls was just what they'd wanted me to do. They were anxious for a reason to escalate things. By speaking up for myself I had fallen into their trap. As the girls approached me, I noticed one was smoking a cigarette, which she flicked on me as soon as they got close. I couldn't believe what was happening. As a result, words were exchanged between the three of us and the moment became heated. I stepped towards the girl who had flicked the cigarette. The other girl stepped between us, stating, "You'll have to fight me first before you fight my sister."

She then bent down and picked up a beer bottle that was lying near the curb. She smacked it on the edge of the curb, breaking the bottom off and then pointed the sharp-edged piece of the broken bottle towards me, making it clear that she was willing to use it on me.

By then, Shereese and her friends were close enough to see what was going on. They all started yelling to get the girls' attention as they ran up to us. By that time I had zoned out. I wasn't worried about the cigarette being flicked on me, or being cut up by a broken glass bottle. All I was focused on was fighting back as my mother had influenced me to do.

That day I was blessed to walk away from a situation that may have landed me in the hospital, or much worse, in my grave at a very early age. That was only the beginning of the many troubles and struggles I had to face. I know momma was doing her best to provide for us but my experience in our new neighborhood was a descent into darkness. A darkness that by this time included exposure to domestic violence, physical abuse and being bullied not only in school, but also within the community. My anger was festering. Add to that, I knew that if I failed to stick up for myself I would have to deal with the physical punishment that my mother would inflict upon me, so my solution in handling my mounting issues was to literally fight back.

The physical altercations I became involved in occurred so frequently that I grew to become extremely exhausted from having to fight so much and it sure didn't help that these altercations where increasing in intensity.

In the fourth grade I got into my very first fight with a classmate named Sophia, that started over a note I was passing down to a friend. Sophia intercepted the note, opened it and read it out loud. I was so embarrassed, not to mention infuriated. Reading my personal note out loud to the entire class was not something I would be forgiving about. As far as I was concerned, I had no choice but to retaliate.

As soon as school ended, I gathered some of my schoolmates, letting all of them know there was going to be a fight. I caught up with Sophia across the street from the school, pushing her from behind to get her attention. I'd been taught not to throw the first punch, but this was a day I would set my own rules. Sophia had pissed me off and my anger was no longer simmering. It had point blank boiled over.

I didn't allow Sophia to respond at that point and no longer cared about her reasoning for reading my note out loud in front of the other students. I had already made up my mind that she was going to pay, not only for intercepting my letter, but also for all of the physical abuse I had to endure, the teasing I was subjected to and the spankings I received by momma for allowing others to hurt me. Sophia had embarrassed me and I was not going to allow her or anyone else to get away with hurting or embarrassing me again.

After pushing Sophia down, I blacked out and began attacking her with pure rage. I didn't notice how forcefully I had been beating her until I heard someone yelling, "Please stop! You're going to kill her."

It turned out to be a resident nearby who'd witnessed my attack on Sophia and knew I needed to be stopped. She had come running out of the townhouse located just behind the spot where the physical altercation occurred. As she approached us, I managed to snap out of my fugue. I noticed Sophia curled up in a fetal position on the sidewalk with her hands tightly braced against her face in an attempt to protect herself from my assault.

Without a word, I gathered my belongings and walked off with my friends while the lady reached down to help Sophia up. At that moment I felt on top of the world; a new world that I had learned to build up on my own. I just knew my mother would be proud of me for sticking up for myself.

My sense of power was short lived. My fight with Sophia cost me my relationship with a very special friend. Her name was Jean and she was the one my note was originally intended for. Jean happened to be Sophia's next door neighbor and their mothers were friends, so when Jean's mother heard about the fight, she forbade Jean from ever playing with me again.

Jean was very sweet, kind and understanding and had been my friend throughout all of the bullying I had endured at the school, so losing her friendship was huge for me. Unfortunately, I managed to gain new friends in Jean's place who were excited by my rage and quite often involved in troubling situations of their own.

By the time I had reached middle school, I had established an undesired record for fighting. Consequently, I was also quite often a target. It was around this time in my life when fights stopped being hand-to-hand. Students were resorting to bringing weapons to school, a development I wasn't equipped to handle.

On one occasion, I was confronted by a girl who was once my friend. For whatever reason, she'd suddenly decided she no longer wanted to share a friendship with me. I never understood what caused her to set her sights on me, but there she was following me home from school one day, telling me that she wanted to fight. When I finally grew tired of her taunting me I agreed to fight with her. As she removed her jacket I noticed that she was carrying a wooden club. It was hanging from her shoulder by a corded rope and the club had a metal tip on the end.

This was brand new territory for me. Using my better judgment I ran as fast as I could. I knew I was capable of out running her to avoid being beaten with that club. I never had to deal with her again, but my problems continued to fester with other students in the school.

Shortly after that I had another, more serious run-in with a much older boy named Tank who attended the same school. Tank was heavily involved in gang activity and a troublemaker who spent most of his time getting suspended from school. Early on in our cordial relationship Tank often referred to me as his "Little sister", until he also turned on me.

Unfortunately, Tank wanted to take our friendship further. He let me know he wanted me as his girlfriend. I didn't have the slightest interest in him beyond our friendship, so I made my best efforts to reject any of the approaches he made towards me.

Tank was not one to take rejection well, so he started a rumor that we were actually dating as a means to save face. I, of course, when I heard the rumor, emphatically denied it. This did nothing but piss Tank off. Not only was he put off at my refusal to date him, now he was embarrassed by his lie being exposed. All of that was too much and he decided to come after me. He felt I was making him look bad by disrespecting him. That was something he was NOT going to tolerate.

I had just arrived to school and was waiting outside of my classroom for the first bell of the day to ring. One of my friend's named Maurice ran up to me and told me that Tank was coming down the hall to fight me. About that time, I noticed Tank barreling down the hallway towards me. The look on his face was all business. As he approached me he began yelling about how I was making him look like a fool, referring to the lies and rumors he had been spreading about me and demanded that I go along with whatever he said about me.

Once he got close enough, he balled up his fists and started throwing punches towards me. Everything was happening so quickly that I didn't have time to think. Once again, I had a quick flash of my mother beating my tail if I allowed Tank to overpower me, so my first instinct was to fight back as hard as I possibly could.

Tank was much taller than I was, so I fought with all my might. The fight led from the hallway to the inside of my classroom. It took two teachers to stop the fight, each one earning a few hits themselves as they struggled to pull us apart. The students in the classroom were in shock. So many of them were afraid of Tank. They were quite surprised that a girl stood up to and fought a guy who many of the students perceived as the most powerful bully in the school.

After the fight, Tank's reputation took a definite hit. All of the students were talking about how a girl "Whooped Tank's ass." If he had been angry with me before, these new rumors took it to a dangerous level.

Tank and I were both suspended. Neither of us were allowed to return to school until our parents attended a meeting with school officials. My mother met with the school principal the very next day and I was permitted to return to school following a few days' suspension. Tank, however never returned to school as a student. Instead, he arrived to school a few days later to taunt and harass me...with a gun.

I did not pay Tank any attention and had gone about my walk home as best I could. Tank was following about a half block behind with a large group of boys who were walking with him. I'd gone about my usual routine, meeting up with the friends I normally walked home with, still paying him no mind.

We'd made it about a third of the way to my home when we heard a noise that sounded much like a firework. We all assumed that Tank was throwing fireworks at us in an attempt to get our attention. I didn't think much of it until one of the girls I was walking with yelled, "He's got a gun!"

My friends scattered, leaving me walking alone. Tank ran up to me, then wrapped his arm around my neck and put the gun to the side of my head. He threatened to shoot me if I tried to call for help.

Once again, I felt as if things were happening in fast motion. I hadn't even considered crying out. All I could think of was the fact that I was just thirteen years old, as I wondered how and why this was happening to me?

Suddenly, Tank lowered the gun from my head and dropped it on the ground. A woman had just pulled up to the stop sign in her car as I calmly continued on with my walk home. After she drove off, Tank picked the gun up from the ground and continued to follow me. I kept walking at a steady pace to show him that I was not afraid of what he would do. In my mind however, I was enraged. Tank had taken a cheap shot by using a weapon to threaten me.

When I made it home, I was furious and brushed past my mother with tears streaming down my face. I went straight to our kitchen to try and find something that I could use as a weapon against Tank. Momma stopped me, asking me to tell her what was wrong. I could barely get the story out, but as soon as I did, momma told me to stay put and she immediately set out to look for Tank. Thankfully, she didn't find him because Tank did not have a care in the world about anyone. I shudder at the thought of what might have happened to momma had she indeed found him.

It was during those few moments while mom was out looking for Tank, that I realized I no longer had a desire to physically fight for survival. The entire violent game of fighting was growing way more serious than what I was able to handle. It had never been a safe option for me to physically protect myself in the first place, but now that weapons had been introduced into the mix, I was taking on even more of a risk.

That single incident had left me severely traumatized and in tears. Momma taught me to stick up for myself by fighting, but she didn't teach me about handling situations that involved the use of guns, which were much more dangerous than wooden clubs. While I was able to escape from being beaten with a club, it was evident that I would not be able to outrun a bullet. I still thank God to this day that Tank didn't shoot me in his attempt to demonstrate his toughness.

Fighting had become a major part of my life that I knew would be a struggle to completely stop, but I also had a desire to live and during that time my life seemed to be flashing before me. It wasn't long before I began to see the light shining at the end of the tunnel. A light that would appear to be so far away, but also a light that would offer me a glimmer of hope. I just had to witness **A World Full of Hate.**

8

A World Full of Hate

"Happiness is in the eye of the beholder" is what I've always heard, but I'd learned it wasn't always that easy to maintain that happiness after moving into the only property available to us in the area of what is now considered the "Gentrified" community of the Five Points. During the time I resided in the historical Five Points area, I found that many of the neighborhood kids weren't very friendly and in fact, some were just down right mean. When I noticed how unhappy many of the kids were, I realized there wasn't much for me to even be happy about.

Many of us residing within the community were experiencing financial struggles, while others were living in poverty. Finding family togetherness was also rare. But there was one family in particular that maintained a strong bond and modeled the true happiness of beholders and they were the Gaines Family. Their brother, Gus was the only boy and oldest brother to three sisters, named Sandra, Shayna and Yolanda. They were the nicest and most cordial family ever and each of the siblings impacted my life in so many positive ways, primarily through the genuine love and care they displayed towards others. Having the ability to spend time with my friends served as an outlet for much of the pain I had learned to suppress. I honestly cannot imagine how life might have turned out for me without the involvement of the Gaines Family in my life. They were definitely a God-sent family.

The Gaines Family resided just up the block from where we lived, coincidentally, in some additional property that my grandfather owned, so I always felt a very special connection with them.

Whenever I would walk through the neighborhood alley, I'd usually see Shayna and Yolanda, the two younger sisters playing outside and they always appeared to be enjoying themselves.

After meeting Shayna, Yolanda and their older siblings, I attached to my new friends like a magnet that was hooked on for life. I basically invited myself into their family of happiness and togetherness. I had adopted this family and was completely absorbed by the love and joy I felt whenever I was around them. They shared so much love for one another and were all genuinely kind-spirited. The strong family bond they shared was one I hadn't really been fully exposed to, realizing that I needed just that in my life in order to overcome so much of the darkness I frequently felt around me. The Gaines Family was a true family and one of the few families that resided in the neighborhood with family values and strong qualities. The bond I established with my new friends had become so strong that there was no other force that could break it. I had found true heaven with the friendship I shared with the Gaines children. Then one summer day they broke the news to me that they were moving to California and that was the day my world began to crumble.

After learning that my best friends were planning to move away indefinitely, I could not stand the thought of being pulled away from them and they understood quite well. They invited me to travel to California with them for the summer and I tried my hardest to find a way to leave with my friends, but it just never worked out. Momma broke the sad news to me that I would not be able to travel to California with my best friends, so I was forced to say farewell, not knowing if I'd ever see them again. Then, that very awful and dreadful day came and they left without me. I had absolutely no idea how I'd spend my free time once they were gone because I didn't have as close of a relationship with any other family in the neighborhood the way I had with the Gaines girls. Whenever I was around them, I experienced life as a child and created many fun times.

After they left, I didn't go outside much and felt so alone and depressed. I eventually started hanging out more with the other kids in the neighborhood and that is when my life seemed to turn into complete hell. I always desired to have caring friends, but I soon realized that the "friends" I had did not care about me in the same manner and were just down right cruel.

Momma would often say, "Those aren't your friends Dionne", whenever I'd get caught up in some kind of trouble with them and it hurt so bad. I tried so hard to develop the same relationship with other kids that I had established with the Gaines girls but it just didn't work. I never quite understood why I wasn't liked very well, or what I had done to trigger such disloyal behavior from others, but it happened and I always seemed to be center stage, getting caught up in so much trouble.

Momma noticed that the kids were doing devious things behind my back, while pretending to be my friends and I just couldn't see it. The kids I had allowed in my circle certainly didn't have the genuinely kind spirit that the Gaines Family displayed towards me. All I knew was I just needed some friends regardless of the cost or whatever was at stake, which I later grew to regret.

During my attempt to have new friends after suffering the loss of the Gaines girls, I began to see and understand more of what momma had been telling me all along. Unfortunately, I had fallen in too deep. I had begun associating with more troubled kids in the neighborhood and at one point had joined along with some other girls who were attempting to organize a girls' gang. Our efforts and attempts never really survived past the initial point, but the guys in our neighborhood seemed to take off and gangs were forming all around us and developing at numerous rates.

In addition to all of the other problems occurring in my neighborhood, I began to notice more of a racial division within our community. The community I resided in was predominately Black and Hispanic, extending from the Five Points down to the projects, so anytime White's moved into the area they were automatically perceived as "rich" and became victims of break-ins, sometimes during broad daylight.

As a small child, I had frequently heard during the late 70's and early 80's, "It's a White man's world" from many adults I was exposed to and this created somewhat of a barrier for me after noticing that many of the commercials advertised between the shows I watched seemed to be happy White people. There weren't many commercials that included Black people unless it was an advertisement of popular Black shows called *Good Times* and *Sanford and Son*, which portrayed the lives of many Blacks who were struggling to survive during that era in time. Many of those shows told it like it was with no sugar coating, so they were definitely shows we, as a community could relate to. Then we had the popular show called *The Jefferson's* about a family "Moving on up" to a better lifestyle and having to deal with racism in the process, so that was truly the world I lived in and there seemed to be very little hope for the true success of minorities residing in the community I was growing up in, which created a very dark and bleak perception for many, especially in consideration of the volume of violence and drugs that were spreading amongst our community.

During my earlier school years, true happiness within the school population seemed to not exist. While the majority of us came from the Five Points and projects, others we considered as the fortunate students were bussed from other areas much further away from the location of our school. Their lives seemed glorious and so much safer, as compared to the lives of many of us who resided within the radius of the school zone. For me, my perception of it was that the children bussed to our school had an outlet to escape whenever they were transported by bus back to their homes.

Surprisingly, by the time I reached middle school, the governor of the city at the time had enrolled his son and daughter in the same school and they seemed to fit right in and breeze through happily, without anyone ever bothering them. They lived in the Colorado Governor's Mansion and definitely had more of a carefree lifestyle. I was told on a few occasions that many of the White kids were actually cool with the minorities in the school and often invited them to what was referred to as "Toga Parties" back then. I was never invited and always believed it was due to my involvement in trouble. My mind at the time was so boxed in, so it was difficult for me to comfortably associate with the Whites who attended the school anyway.

At the end of every school year it was a ritual for many of the troublemakers in the school to select other students to "jump", so it was a common practice to be prepared just in case you became the target, but one year in particular was different.

The majority of the years, it was most common for the Black students to fight with one another, but this one year the most influential student in the school decided to lead a group and target some of the White kids who resided in the area near the school. This was the first time I ever witnessed racism at our school and it was a struggle for me to process at such a young age.

The leader of the group suggested that they jump one of the "rich" White kids and the group of boys happened to target a White girl walking home from school. The boys snatched specific jewelry items off that they believed were of value, as they pushed, shoved and punched at her. In an effort to protect herself, she shielded her face with her books. As I passed by, I noticed the leader of the group snatch her watch from her wrist. I was so saddened by what I witnessed and did not realize until that moment how angry so many of the youth in our community were that I was surrounded by.

By the following year, many of the boys from our middle school who took part in the attack against that girl had joined gangs and the leader remained in his role. Some years later, the gangs broke off and multiplied into subdivisions, leading into what was known in our streets as the "Summer of Violence", which grew to become a very huge issue in our state and that is the time when I started losing many childhood friends and schoolmates to incarceration and death.

I began to notice the true struggle for what it was worth, realizing there was no way out for many who became succumbed to the violence in the streets. Many of the young souls were left to learn how to survive on their own, with very little foundation or guidance offered from within their homes. I happened to be one of those lost souls, desiring the need for protection as I struggled to survive on my own. My only hope and desire was to succeed since I had already become caught up in the battle of fighting to survive. After our unsuccessful and short-lived attempt to organize our girls gang had fallen through the cracks, I quickly came to my senses and decided against pursuing the gang life as a means of protection and survival and therefore, backed away fast from becoming involved.

One thing I didn't completely back away from was dating the guys from my neighborhood that had joined gangs. I had learned how to keep my relationships with the boys who seemed to stay in trouble on the "down low" from momma, but it wasn't long before she found out.

I had a boyfriend named J.M. and although he was a gang member, he was actually very sweet. J.M. and I shared a tight bond and we really genuinely cared for one another. We spent many nights talking on the phone and visiting one another as often as we were able to. Around that time, I started to notice that many of my friends and former schoolmates from middle school were disappearing from the streets and eventually learned they were actually being removed from their homes as a result of their delinquent behavior. Many were being sent to neighborhood placement agencies and detention centers and J.M. was one of them. In fact, one of the barbed wire detention centers happened to be located within walking distance from the home that we lived in.

I never found out what delinquent activity J.M. engaged in that caused him to be removed from his home, but he ended up committed by the state to a detention center in La Junta, CO for what seemed like eternity. Over time, J.M. and I were able to reconnect through snail mail and spent a lot of time writing letters back and forth to one another, which worked out well until momma intercepted one of the letters and started yelling at me about it one day, asking me why I was writing a boy from La Junta, CO. Momma ripped my letter open as she was yelling at me, removed it from the envelope and began reading the letter out loud. That is when she realized J.M. and I were in a relationship. Momma ripped the letter up and forbade me from having any further contact with J.M., so our efforts made in maintaining a connection through writing had come to an abrupt end. I was so sad and heartbroken because I knew J.M. and I relied on one another for support to get through the madness that we were both surrounded by.

I continued to carry on without having any further contact with J.M. and moved on with my life. Years later, I happened to be walking down a street towards my grandfather's rental business one day and J.M. called out my name from the porch of a home he happened to be at and ran over to me. J.M. told me he was living with his girlfriend who had recently delivered their baby girl. I was happy to hear the news that he had settled down and we both were extremely happy to see one another and catch up after growing apart. After our conversation, J.M. and I parted ways and that was the last time I saw J.M. alive.

A few years later I heard that J.M. had just been released from jail and was out partying at a club with some friends when he encountered problems with some rival gang members. Words were exchanged and the verbal altercation was carried out into the streets. As the story was relayed to me, after the club ended, some of the party-goers decided to travel to another party that was going on. J.M. happened to be in one of the cars with his friends and the rival gang members in another. The car with two well-known gang members began chasing J.M. and his friend. When they caught up to them the rival gang members fired multiple gun shots. J.M. was killed.

This was so sad for me and hit so close to home because J.M. was someone I really cared about. Equally as tragic, another person I cared about was involved. A young man named Edwin had been with the guys who fired the gun. Edwin was family, as he happened to be Benny's cousin. By then, Benny and I had been dating for a few years, throughout my high school and early adult years. Benny was also the father of my first child, so Edwin and I had grown to know one another quite well. How would I ever explain to my son that his blood relative had been involved in the murder of someone so dear to my heart?

J.M.'s life was lost and Edwin and his two gang affiliated friends were all sentenced to life in prison without the possibility of parole and that was how it ended; a lifetime of hurt over the loss of a sweet friend and a dear family member.

After J.M.'s death, I spent a lot of time reflecting on my elementary and middle school years. I vividly recall standing between an apartment building located across the street from my school, smoking marijuana with two schoolmates before heading over to the school. As we were standing there sharing the joint, I clearly heard the words, "You won't make it to see the age of 18 if you don't change your life." It was a very uneasy feeling that came over me and frankly, quite scary. It was at that moment that I decided I did not want to lose my life as a result of the unhealthy choices I had been making and made a vow to fight the battle at all costs to remain alive.

I had no idea where that voice was coming from, but it was loud and clear in my head and it was at that time that I knew I was headed down a very dark road of destruction with no way of returning or escaping. The kids in the neighborhood had begun turning their backs on me and many of the fights I was dealing with were becoming way more serious and seemed to be occurring in clusters. At one point during a fight I engaged in with a girl I thought was my friend, I nearly got my eye knocked out by the heel of her boot that she had hit me with. This was one of the girls that momma would constantly warn me about that I failed to take heed to.

The word was out that many others I also thought of as friends were planning to come after me and I felt completely unsafe and trapped. I had finally allowed momma's words to sink in and I was convinced that the ones I thought were my friends, actually weren't. All of the signs were quite evident. I just had the tough job of seeing it for what it really was. My world turned cold.

After finally accepting the truth, momma began networking with a leader from the church we attended, who was also an educator at a school with a much better reputation than the school I was attending and encountering so many problems at. This caring teacher was truly an angel that I will always believe was placed in my path to assist me in escaping much of the hateful behaviors that were projected towards me by so many of my peers. I know he knew and understood the struggles I was experiencing.

By transferring, I was able to escape from what I perceived as pure hell, although I still had to return to the same environment after catching the city bus home from school. It just helped that I didn't have to attend the same school where I was disliked by so many. I was provided with an outlet for change to be made possible… a second chance at another school where I was treated with an enormous amount of respect by other kids who appeared much happier and friendlier towards one another. My troubles with my peers had finally begun to taper off and it was a safe feeling. By the time I entered high school, I began to encounter a separate set of issues, which involved the death of my grandfather when I was 16 years old.

Grandpa had been battling cancer for a while, but it was kept on the down low for so long that I didn't find out until he was gravely ill, with very little weight as he sat in his hospital bed with a severely swollen tongue. He couldn't eat, drink or speak much and seemed to have no recollection of who I was near the end of his days. In fact, momma relayed to me that he frequently called her Beatrice; her stepsister's name, which hurt momma a lot, considering the fact that they weren't ever close. Grandpa meant the world to me and had been the primary push in my motivation to attend church on Sunday mornings when I was a child, by knocking on our door and offering to pay me a dollar if I agreed to attend church with him. If I allowed grandpa to persuade me, I would earn an extra dollar to place in the offering tray. I enjoyed earning money because that dollar stretched a long way. I'd either spend it on candy or playing video games. Grandpa was setting the foundation at an early age that filtered over into my young adult years as a young single mom. Attending church during my early 20's contributed to savoring my sanity.

Grandpa's life had come to an end and he wasn't even recognizable at the time of his death. Grandpa was a very strong and healthy looking man with a stern demeanor about him. He also had the most beautiful hazel eyes. Unless he was fussing about something, his typical demeanor was very sweet and caring. Losing grandpa was a very sad time in my life. He cared so deeply for his grandchildren and definitely was a family man. He was the type of man who had high expectations of his children and grandchildren and desired for all to succeed.

He was also an entrepreneur and ran his rental business well and all of that came to an end on the day he took his final breath. Grandpa passed away a couple of days prior to my sixteenth birthday and I had the pleasure of being a part of his passing. Momma made it a mission to remain by his side during his final days and hours. Shereese was residing out of state at the time, but happened to call home one night to see how he was doing. I told Shereese that momma was at the hospital with our grandpa and used our three-way calling service to contact momma so we could check in on his condition.

When momma answered the phone, she relayed to us that grandpa was coming close to taking his final breath. Momma paused for a moment as Shereese and I silently held on the line. Momma quietly stated, "He's gone… he took his final breath" and that was the end of my grandfather. The one who provided us with a place to stay so we could move out of the safe house; the one who would always knock on door early Sunday mornings to encourage me to attend church with him; the one who was positive, inspiring and truly left a legacy behind for future generations to follow. Grandpa left me with such deep and fond memorable moments that I will forever cherish. He had passed on to a place where there was no more pain and suffering.

Days following grandpa's death, I experienced an outburst in school after my math teacher, Mr. Gefford tossed my homework at me for failing to record my name on my work. I was under a lot of stress and rushing to complete my work in order to turn it in early, in preparation of attending my grandpa's funeral. Mr. Gefford's actions and lack of respect caused me to explode in front of the entire class during my sophomore year. I walked up and shoved him in his chest with both of my hands, as I yelled "My grandfather just died!" before storming out of the school and walking home.

My anger had once again gotten the best of me. The death of my grandfather also wore my mother's strength down. All of the family moments that we'd shared, with momma cooking fried chicken and storing it in her stone cookware every Saturday morning before we headed down to hang out at grandpa's rental business where we spent many of our Saturdays. There was nothing more comforting than those fond memories of family togetherness. Grandpa's death caused our entire family to divide and there were many angry family members. Our family was in complete turmoil and it was so bad that momma heard a rumor spreading within our family that someone was planning to blow up the church where grandpa's funeral was scheduled to be held. We never found out whether any of this information was true, but one situation that was unfortunate for mom and her living siblings was the fact that all had been excluded from grandpa's Living Will.

As a side gig, my Uncle Duke and Uncle Darren ran a barbershop that was attached to the rental property owned by my grandfather, and after his passing my step grandmother cut everyone off. She had stripped every bit of property away from grandpa's living children and during the same time my uncles lost their barbershop, we lost our housing. My step grandmother didn't waste any time to slapping an eviction notice on our front door and it was devastating because we had no place to go. This had become our safe haven after moving out of the safe house and here we were again facing homelessness and this time, grandpa was not around to rescue us.

Uncle Duke and Uncle Darren turned their sorrow into motivation and set out to follow their dream and passion by locating another spot to get their barbershop business up and running again. Unfortunately, that dream for my uncles was cut short. Two weeks after my grandfather died, Uncle Duke got killed in a freak car accident.

The way the story was relayed to my mother, Uncle Duke had picked up my Aunt Norma from the school she worked at and they were headed back home, down a dark road in the country where they lived. As they were traveling towards their home, a driver of a trailer-type hauling vehicle was traveling in the opposite direction with some sort of tractor on top that had finger blades hanging off the sides of the truck. As Uncle Duke passed alongside of the other driver's truck, the finger blades of the tractor cut down into the hood of the automobile, grinding through the hood of Uncle Duke's automobile and tragically splitting his head open. Auntie Norma was not injured in the accident and only heard the grinding noise of the blades cutting into the automobile they were in before realizing what had happened. Uncle Duke was dead at the scene, his life cut so short.

From my understanding, there was a law set into place at the time that required individuals to use red trailer safety flags to alert other drivers when there were extended parts being hauled, which the other driver did not have attached to the tractor he was transporting. Considering the way the accident occurred, I am not convinced that the flags would have even made a difference because the roads were so dark to travel on to begin with. It just seems like it was his time to go. With my Uncle Duke's sudden and tragic loss, there was no way to prepare for his death. We were still grieving the loss of my grandfather and now he was joined by one of his son's.

After Uncle Duke's death, momma had become even more furious, feeling betrayed by the one family member I always considered as a grandma, although step. There seemed to be no genuine love involved.

As a family experiencing severe trauma, this woman I always respected and considered as my grandmother, although step, seemed to have no concern in the world for our safety and wellbeing. Momma's stress level as a single mother struggling to make ends meet by working three jobs had hit its peak.

The day came that momma was forced to vacate the premises of grandpa's once owned property. Momma reached out to her friends and through God's grace, one of her friend's knew someone who owned vacant property. Our new home was a tiny white house with a flat roof and wasn't in the best condition, but it was a place for us to call home.

After being evicted, there was no further contact with my step-grandmother and I was permitted by momma to disregard her by the title I had referred to her as all of my life. My perception of her had developed more into that of an enemy of evil doings that destroyed what little bit of a family we had left after grandpa's passing. There was no willing soul available to help mold the pieces together.

Including momma, there were three of the five siblings still living. Her eldest brother lived in California and although her only other living brother was local, the contact they shared was rare. The entire family grew distant and became more like strangers to one another.

There were times a few of my cousins would attempt to reconnect with our family in an effort to reestablish our family bond, but momma just wouldn't allow it to happen and instead, placed us in pure isolation. Momma had an extremely difficult time facing and accepting her own dark past and when my cousins would make attempts to obtain information relating to our family history, momma would completely shut down and display an angry demeanor, all as a result of the pain and guilt she lived with every single day of her life. Momma's disappointments seemed to cut so deep into her flesh that the wounds from her past never healed.

The remainder of my teen years were extremely difficult without my grandfather. There was just no support or involvement with my maternal relatives, so momma's focus was solely on us as a family unit.

My outlet in surviving through all of this chaotic turmoil was having the presence of Benny in my life. Although I still struggled a great deal with the darkness that seemed to haunt me for so very long, I continued to make gradual progress toward my effort in becoming a new and changed person.

Although quite devastating for momma, it turned out to be a true blessing for me that we were evicted out of our home in the Five Points community. I certainly had no complaints. I just didn't have the ability to openly express my true feelings to momma because I knew she would be devastated, especially due to the circumstances of the traumatic events that led up to us being displaced.

After all we had been through as a family, I knew that I was responsible for living my life in a manner that was meaningful for me and for that reason, had to learn to live it in the best way I knew possible. Momma would frequently tell me that I would not amount to anything in life and that my life would be just like hers, which I refused to accept.

Momma tried so hard to provide me with the similar life-style that I had before she allowed Hades into our lives, but so much damage had already been caused and it sure didn't help during the times that momma would emotionally put me down because I had embarrassed her by my early pregnancy. I would always think to myself that having a baby would not stop me from attending college and successfully making it in life and sure wasn't going to accept the fact that having a baby meant my life was completely over. I witnessed and learned from so many of the mistakes momma had made, even though I still ended up heading down the same path she had taken a few times in my life. I knew life would be harder, but I had strong hope, belief and faith in my ability to succeed while working hard to accomplish my goals, which I later perceived and comprehended as **A Glimmer of Hope**.

9

A Glimmer of Hope

Outside of my family trauma, I lived in a community where so many families were experiencing similar struggles with poverty, drugs and violence. Gangs became more prevalent in my neighborhood which of course, led to an eruption of street violence. Many of my former classmates and friends were getting killed on a regular basis. It was a sad period for me to witness many of the lives of so many young men and women ending so soon, and there seemed to be absolutely nothing that could be done about it.

Momma tried to do the best she could with what she had and although she didn't always have the money, she still seemed to find a way to provide for us. I had developed a good friendship with a girl named Sierra who persuaded me to join a community drill team with her, but I soon found out that the uniforms and drill team boots were quite expensive. Momma ordered the boots and pulled out her sewing machine, studied the pattern of the uniform I needed and made my uniform so I could participate in the drill team meets and parades. Although short-lived, that turned out to be one of the greatest highlights of my life. Another outside activity momma exposed me to as a child was ballet, through a community recreation center when I was six years old, but that experience was short-lived as well. I quit shortly after my sister, Shereese decided to quit. Ballet didn't seem to be for either one of us.

Momma sure did find ways to break through barriers to get us involved whenever she was able and that included doing everything in her willpower to straighten out the crooked path I was traveling down. Part of her plan included sending me back to a faith-based private school.

By the end of my eighth-grade year it was just me, Jeris and momma in the house. Shereese had moved out of the house shortly after graduating from high school. Momma worked three jobs to earn enough money to cover the costs of our family needs and also the tuition she was preparing to pay for me to return the Catholic school system. She had made up her mind that she would do whatever was necessary to provide me with a better future in life.

I was excited to move on to high school, however, not so excited about the school momma was preparing to send me to. Most of my friends and acquaintances were headed off to our community home school where momma refused to allow me to attend, as a result of the struggles I had encountered. Near the end of my eighth grade year, momma had taken her first step in creating and stabilizing change for me by reaching out to Mr. Duncan, a school educator and member of the church we attended.

Mr. Duncan taught eighth grade at a well-known middle school, located much further away from the school I attended. To get to school each day, I would have to take two city buses and that made no difference to momma as long as I was safe. Momma worked diligently alongside of Mr.

Duncan, who served as my advocate to help get me enrolled at the same school where he taught. The networking between the two of them was strong in their push for me to enter a new door of opportunity. Momma explained to me that the school she had arranged to send me to for the last three months of eighth grade was located in a much safer community with new kids and fewer problems.

She was honest in explaining to me that the principal of the new school was quite reluctant to approve my enrollment, for fear that I would bring problems into the school, but momma had assured him that there would be no problems and with that, my hardship transfer to my new middle school was approved. I was granted the opportunity for a much fresher ending to my middle school years.

My transition into my new school turned out to be very positive and was certainly more of a healthier experience than what I had experienced at my last school. The kids at the school appeared to be mature in the sense of being less drama-filled and also portrayed more of a kind-spirited demeanor, with more of a love for life. The environment was indeed much safer and my experience was certainly more positive than the environment I had come from. I completed my final three months of middle school without any problems and was finally on my way to high school.

After school let out for the summer, my father had arranged a trip for me to travel to Washington D.C. to spend time with his late brother's family who I had never met. I spent a few weeks living with my aunt and cousins and created memorable experiences with my family. They took time out of their busy work schedules to show me around town. We visited the White House, Smithsonian Museum and I was also blessed with the opportunity to see and hear the former boxer, Muhammad Ali speak to a crowd in a park and made sure to capture the moment by snapping many pictures of him.

This was certainly exposure to a much better lifestyle than the lifestyle I had been living. I spent time playing with my younger cousins and we even got into some trouble after I allowed them to talk me into watching a movie they knew they had no business watching. I remember them staring at me as they anxiously waited to see my reaction to an inappropriate part of the movie, which caught me by surprise. It was something we all giggled about, but it wasn't so funny after my cousins returned home and found out that I had allowed my younger cousins to con me into watching a movie that we had no business watching. It was definitely something most kids would do in their effort to have fun.

After returning to Colorado, I was preparing for my return back to the parochial school system. A total of five calendar school years had passed and I realized I would have to make some adjustments to reacclimate myself back into an environment that had become unfamiliar. I had become accustomed to the larger schools with many more students and didn't like the idea of attending a much smaller school with so few students, but momma refused to allow me to return to the public school system, constantly reminding me that I would be killed if she allowed me to return to school with the kids I had encountered so many problems with. Momma had finally realized the hell I had been living in and decided that she would do any and everything she possibly could to keep me alive and away from the kids that seemed to hate me for no apparent reason.

My first day of high school had arrived. We were still residing in the Five Points area, so it took two city buses for me to commute to my new school. The environment was altogether different than the environment I had come from. Some of the sweetest moments entailed reuniting with kids I had attended elementary school with during my early years. It seemed that all of the kids in the school were super nice and what caught me off-guard the most, was when the entire class would say "Bless you" whenever I sneezed. This was definitely a huge difference for me in consideration of the evil world I had been exposed to, but it was all for the better. I actually felt true love and concern from my peers in the school. Within six months of attending the school, I had begun to transform and had become well-adapted to the change. I still had my violent tendencies, but it wasn't nearly as bad as it was during my late elementary and middle school years. This period in my life was the start of my ability to see a glimmer of light in my new world that provided hope and more of a positive future.

Socially, the new, quieter environment became difficult for me to navigate. I was finding it hard to fit in with a peer group I felt I could relate to. Many of my schoolmates were residing with both of their parents in immaculate homes that were located in really nice areas. A great portion of the parents were well-to-do business owners who thought nothing of gifting their kids with luxury vehicles for their sixteenth birthdays.

My life, in comparison, was much different. There was no fancy car in my future and due to the fact that momma didn't even own a car, I knew the city bus was how it was going to be for me throughout my high school years. Momma's income from the three jobs she was working was barely enough to make ends meet, let alone, pay the high cost tuition for me to attend the private school she had enrolled me in. Momma also had to make sure I had enough bus fare to get back and forth to school. I am not sure whether or not momma allowed my father to help pay my tuition, but almost certain it was something she desired to do on her own.

I returned home in an angry mood most days, still begging my mother to withdraw me from the private school system. I would try my hardest to convince her that she was working too hard and wasting her money, but she just wouldn't budge. Momma stood strong to her word, still reminding me that if she allowed me to attend the high school where many of my old friends and enemies were, many of those same kids would more than likely end up killing me, so I was stuck. Unfortunately, many of my old habits were still very much a part of my life and I periodically fell back on them in order to create a more familiar environment.

I managed to find a crowd of friends to hang with outside of my high school environment, creating a new life of my own. I had slyly found a way to migrate back to many of my old ways with this outgoing group of teenagers, causing many of my past behaviors to become unveiled in some of the worst ways possible. I seemed to attract and become accustomed to being with a wild high school crowd. Hanging with them made me feel as if I was living the most satisfying life; a life full of binge drinking, drug experimentation and sexual promiscuity. My new life felt all too familiar to the past life I was used to living, but the new kids I was hanging with were simply just high school partiers looking for the perfect opportunity to have fun. This was also the time that I met my high school sweetheart, Benny.

Benny and I met at a dance club that I attended with my friend, Cadence, during the start of my freshman year. He was a very nice young man; almost too nice compared to many of the boys I had dated in my past. Benny became my anchor during the course of my high school years.

I had a lot of anger built up inside from the past abuse and trauma I had endured. A lot of my embedded anger was primarily aimed at men as a result of how momma had been treated. I soon came to realize that my trust in men and relationships was shattered. I knew I wanted to be in a relationship and have a companion, but I did not know how to develop a healthy relationship, after everything I had witnessed.

Benny was a soft and kind-spirited young man who loved and cared so deeply for me and in return, suffered the brunt of my embedded, suppressed anger that lived and festered inside of me.

Even though my mother struggled financially in her effort to get me back on track with exposure to a healthier lifestyle, the dark cloud hovering over me still existed so vividly, which created severe emotional bouts of explosive anger, jealousy and insecurity. Throughout my relationship with Benny, I had grown accustomed to hurting him in every possible way imaginable.

The love that Benny displayed towards me proved that he was committed to helping me deal with my struggles. I was too young to process what I had been through, or even explain in detail all of the struggles I had experienced. Besides, momma always instructed me to keep our business in our family, which contributed to me bottling up so much pain inside.

All of that combined caused me to have explosive outbursts. During my early teenage years I lived with a desire to hurt and cause physical pain to others, especially Benny. I was just too young at the time to appreciate his kindness and after witnessing momma being beaten so badly, I had vowed that I would not allow any man to ever put his hands on me and instead would become the perpetrator of abuse in my relationship. I would be the one to cause my victim to pay for every bit of mistreatment that I had endured in my past.

I wasn't so loyal to Benny and many of times took detours from our established relationship, often running back to Benny who always seemed to have his arms open for my return. Our relationship had turned dysfunctional and neither of us had the tools to recognize how to face and effectively deal with our relationship struggles. Benny had begun to rescue and enable me in some of the most unhealthiest ways, but he was my primary support in learning to survive through my mental and emotional struggles.

The love that Benny and I shared was extremely deep for one another, but remained unhealthy. We were living a life where it was difficult to be in a relationship and even more difficult to be apart from one another. Benny and I had become entangled in our unhealthy world of a relationship and sadly, we were the only ones with the ability to save ourselves. After nearly four years of binge drinking, turning to whatever drug I could try in an effort to numb my suppressed pain and indulging in sexual promiscuity, life had begun to slow down for us, but my substance abuse was still a very prominent risk factor in my life.

One night, Benny and I had purchased some alcohol to consume, which I guzzled down as Benny was driving around the city. I had become so intoxicated that everything started spinning at an extremely fast pace for me. After realizing my inability to gain control over the matter, I became fearful of the unexpected outcome of my destructive behavior. Benny reclined my seat so I could lean back in order to try and relax, but nothing we tried seemed to work. I was crying and calling out for Benny to help me, but there wasn't much he could do and in turn, Benny started to grow fearful. This was the first time and one of the few times I ever heard Benny cry. I had no idea what was happening, but I desperately wished for it to stop. I forced myself to relax and ended up blacking out for a short time and when I regained consciousness, I realized that the spinning had stopped. This experience was one of the worst experiences I had ever encountered while drinking and unfortunately, alcohol abuse wasn't my only risk factor during those trying times. In addition to alcohol, drugs became an additional risk factor in my life, which led to another close encounter.

I had attended a party that was hosted at a recreational facility where I was employed at the time and that party attracted a large crowd, most of whom were hanging out in the parking lot, socializing. A coworker of mine walked up to me and asked me if I wanted to get high with her and a couple of he friends. Of course, I accepted. She led me to a van parked in the parking lot and we climbed into the back. There were two young men sitting inside. I thought nothing of it when one of them pulled out a very thick joint. He lit it up, took a hit and then passed it around. When it got to me, I took a huge hit. The size of this joint was quite unusual, but I saw it as a free high and certainly didn't question it.

I had already been drinking and acting like quite the fool, so adding another substance only made it worse for me. After we all shared the joint, my coworker and I got out of the van. I had planned on going back to enjoy the party. Suddenly, I started developing a strange feeling that I had never before experienced. I began to feel very light and my actions were completely out of control.

Of course, Benny was there that night and when he realized I was acting different, he started following me around in the parking lot, asking me if I had consumed drugs. Benny was well aware of my struggles with drug usage and would constantly discourage me from using substances in my effort to cope. I appreciated Benny's care and concern, but I knew if I ever made the decision to quit using drugs, that I would need to do it for myself and not anyone else and at that point, I didn't care to stop.

I treated Benny so disrespectfully that night. In addition to yelling at him, I hit him on top of his head with an empty, plastic soda bottle a couple of times in front of the crowd. I yelled at him to leave me alone as I ran off in the opposite direction. Benny was only trying to take care of me but I forcefully rejected all of his attempts in making sure I was alright. Eventually he left and I was transported home by a coworker.

That following Monday when I arrived to work, my friend who had invited me to smoke with her on the night of the party had approached me and told me that her friends who we had smoked the joint with admitted to her that it had been laced with cocaine, which explained much of my out-of-control behavior. The high I experienced that night was a high that I never forgot. I did not like the predicament I had placed myself in and sure did not like the unfamiliar feeling that it gave me. It certainly wasn't a new thing for me to act like a fool when I desired, but this particular night, I had placed myself in the center of the stage and had earned the award and title for the top fool of the night. But despite my behavior, Benny was there to welcome me back into his life.

Benny and I dated off and on throughout high school and during the second half of my senior year, I learned I was pregnant. I was 17 years old. I knew Benny was a good man and even though I didn't always treat him kindly and often felt I didn't deserve him, I knew I wanted to be connected with him for the remainder of my life, so finding out I was pregnant with his child was satisfying.

Although our relationship was not as stable as it could have been and instead, on and off throughout our young years, my pregnancy was the initial contributing factor to me becoming more grounded and responsible in my life. Through his genuine care for me, Benny had gained my trust by sticking with me throughout so many mixed emotions I was experiencing during that period of my life. I certainly wasn't used to being loved and cared for in such a way. Consequently, I had a strong desire to hold on to Benny for life. It was my way of doing what was necessary in my effort of **Breaking Out of Bondage**.

Part 2
Then Came the Light

10

Breaking Out of Bondage

As a young adult, it was imperative for me to make certain I did not repeat the same mistakes as my mother had and I surely had no plans of exposing my children to the abuse of alcohol and drugs. I had made up my mind very early on that I would not subject any child I brought into this world to the pain I had to endure.

Accepting the responsibility of pregnancy was the primary motivator in my decision to refrain from using and abusing substances. At this early stage in my life, I hadn't quite learned about the dangers of repeating cycles. I just knew I wanted to be the best mommy I could possibly be to my unborn child. I knew this little helpless life growing inside of me deserved a chance for a much better life than I had lived up to that point.

The downfall involving my pregnancy was that it wasn't embraced well by others closely involved in my life which created a major strain for me. Of course, momma was the least supportive and I never fully adjusted to her raging anger towards me. Every day my mother had to wake up and see me, she was reminded of what she perceived as another failure in her life. The child she had fought so hard to save and the one she'd sacrificed so much for was now her greatest disappointment. Momma's fight for me had abruptly come to an end and she felt she had lost the battle.

A huge portion of momma's disappointment and raging anger towards me stemmed from her shattered dreams and aspirations for me. Momma wanted me to live the life she had always desired to live for herself and since she wasn't able to successfully attain her own personal goals, her eyes were set on me. Momma had developed strong hopes and dreams of sending me away to college, preferably a historically Black college or university, most commonly known as HBCU, where I could spread my wings even further and see the world. But instead, I had gotten pregnant.

Momma was so furious towards me for dashing her dreams that one evening when she was yelling at me, she allowed her anger to get the best of her. She approached me in an aggressive manner and pushed me, slamming my back up against the wall of our living room. I knew in an instant that momma was making every attempt to cause me to miscarry my unborn child. As my back hit against the wall, I slowly slid down, burying my head into my hands. I cried, while thinking to myself that my pregnancy was over.

If momma hadn't caused me to miscarry that evening, it was for certain bound to happen. I knew I was at stake of losing my unborn child if I chose to remain under the same roof as momma. I was an embarrassment to her, a symbol of her failure. She had sacrificed so much, worked three jobs, and spent the majority of her hard-earned funds to cover the cost for me to attend a private school. She had strong hopes that I would make her proud, just as Aunt Summer had once predicted. But instead of being college bound, she had to deal with the despairing news of my pregnancy, just one semester prior to my graduation from high school.

When Jace found out, he was also extremely disappointed in me and sided with my mother. Together, they applied an enormous amount of pressure on my relationship with Benny, which was enough to push him in the opposite direction. My mother and father did everything imaginable to create and instill fear as Benny and I prepared for the birth of our child.

Both of my parents demanded that I take the steps necessary to arrange child support for the next eighteen years, while presuming that my relationship with Benny wouldn't last. The pressure they applied made it difficult for me to see Benny on a regular basis.

Momma would often yell at me, telling me that my life was going to be just like hers and that there was no future for me. She also told me that I would never be able to attend college as a young single mother with a child. With all of the hurtful words that my mother expressed and the harsh actions of my father, I began to truly fear my ability to raise a child. Benny was also feeling the pressure. Between the two of us, we started believing that the best option was to abort our child. Benny and I seemed to have no one in our corner from either side of our family. Everyone seemed to try and persuade me to get an abortion.

I had no idea if I'd be able to go through with it. I had an initial appointment with momma's Ob-Gyn to confirm my pregnancy. A sonogram was performed and validated that I was seven weeks pregnant. I could see a swift blinking motion which the doctor relayed to me was my baby's heartbeat. I also saw my child's little arms and legs, as the tiny fetus floated around in an uncontrolled manner.

Despite the bond I was already forming with my unborn child, the stress of dealing with momma's anger, my father's disappointment in me, and Benny's growing distance from me, I felt there really was no other option available to me. I followed through, as advised by many, with scheduling the appointment at an abortion clinic. Benny borrowed money from his father in order to pay for the initial appointment.

Benny and I attended the appointment together. Sitting in the waiting room, I felt sad inside and extremely uncertain, not knowing if I was making the right decision for my life as I sat within the walls of the abortion clinic. What I did know was that if I chose to abort my baby based on what everyone else thought was best for me, that my decision would scar me for the remainder of my life.

As Benny and I sat there waiting to be called, I noticed another Black couple sitting just a few seats away. They had a Bible that they appeared to be reading together, each holding up an end. After noticing this, my first thought was to ask myself why they were sitting there if the matter was serious enough for them to be reading the Bible. It was at that point that I began to realize that I wanted nothing to do with aborting my pregnancy. I was going to meet with the clinic's counselor in hopes that I would receive some emotional and mental support.

Instead, when I was called back alone for my counseling session, the young lady was very brief with me. With a tired sounding voice, she asked one question, "Why do you want to have an abortion?" and my response to her was, "Because everyone else wants me to". She responded with, "Okay," as she quickly jotted down some notes on a piece of paper before sending me to the next phase of the process. My initial thought was, *"Well, so much for the emotional and mental support I was seeking."*

Benny was allowed in the room for the next phase. We were informed that I was so far along into my pregnancy that my only option was to allow them to vaginally insert a laminaria seed. The seed would slowly expand to the size of my cervix which would basically begin the slow process of killing the life that was growing inside me. These were truly difficult words to absorb. They advised me that I'd have to return in a few days to deliver my dead fetus.

It just didn't feel right to me. After hearing this, I really struggled to go through with the abortion. Fortunately, the decision was made for me. Benny and I didn't have the full amount of funds at the time to begin the procedure. I used that as my excuse to walk away from a decision everyone else felt was best for my body and my future.

As we walked out of the clinic, I made up my mind that I was not returning and therefore, would learn to deal head on with every bit of hardship I had headed my way as a young, single parent. I also made up my mind that that would be the last time I ever allowed anyone else to dictate the direction my life would take. This would be the beginning of a new journey for me and any further decisions I made would be decisions I would have to live with for the remainder of my life.

I took into strong consideration, the fact that most of the individuals who were attempting to influence my decisions would eventually pass on and I would be left with the question, "What if?", in allowing others to make such a crucial decision for me. I knew terminating my pregnancy with this precious little soul would leave me with an embedded scar that I most likely would've never forgiven myself for.

I ended up turning to one of my friend's I had known since the eighth grade. Her name was Cadence and she attended the school I had transferred to on hardship status at the end of my eighth grade year. Having Cadence as a friend was like a breath of fresh air. In order to provide my unborn child with a chance of survival, I knew I had to move out of my mother's house, so I called Cadence and asked her to pick me up.

No sooner than momma left for work that evening, I began packing my bags. It had been my duty to look after my little brother while momma was at work. That night I walked my brother across the street to a well-known neighbor's home. Our neighbor agreed to keep Jeris until momma returned home from work.

Cadence drove over to pick me up. Once we got to her house, her mom told me that I could live with them for as long as necessary, but I had to call my mother in her presence to tell her where I was. That was the hard part, I really didn't want my mother to know. In a sense, I had run away from home, but I obliged and although tense, the conversation I had with my mother went okay.

After moving in with Cadence, I continued to attend school. I was determined to finish my senior year of high school. Fortunately Cadence lived less than a mile from the location of my high school which made it easy for me to get back and forth. Momma thought I had dropped out, so she stopped paying my tuition. Luckily, when my father found out that I was still attending, he picked up the remaining balance of my tuition and continued making payments throughout the remainder of my school year.

After moving away from my mother, my father provided me with more support. He would stop by to pick me up and take me to the grocery store to purchase food for the household. Daddy also took me to apply for welfare, which provided me with some degree of a foundation as I awaited the birth of my child. Although he could be tough-spirited at times, daddy proved to me that he was a forgiving man and would continue to remain by my side regardless, just as he had promised my mother when I was born.

Daddy had also arranged for me to see his doctor for medical checkups. I will never forget meeting Dr. Jackson for the first time and telling him how much of a disappointment I was to both of my parents, primarily my mother. That is when Dr. Jackson asked me if I knew of a famed track runner who had also become pregnant and given birth to her child at a very early age and rose to fame with her track and field talent. Those words spoken over me by Dr. Jackson provided me with confidence and hope that all would work out. After leaving his office, I had a new sense of pride about me and knew that I needed to do everything in my willpower to continue surviving the storms that were headed my way.

Shortly before I graduated, my sister Shereese traveled back to Denver from Norfolk, VA where she had been living. Shereese talked momma into allowing me to return home, then called to convince me to move back.

The only concern I had was whether or not I'd be safe under the same roof as my mother. By then, I was heading into my sixth month of pregnancy, so my unborn child was my only concern. I wanted to make certain to keep him safe and free from momma attempting to cause harm to me or my baby.

Momma had grown to accept my situation but our relationship was still strained throughout the remainder of my pregnancy and following my baby's birth. For the first time in my life, I stood strong for something that I believed in and refused to allow momma to make decisions for me that I didn't perceive as healthy. In a sense, I had entered a journey of **Reclaiming My Life**.

11

Reclaiming My Life

It was three and a half weeks prior to my due date. Benny was headed over to pick me up so we could hang out for the day. Getting away from the house was therapeutic for me, so I took complete advantage of every opportunity I had. I was quite nervous. I often wondered how I would know my baby was on the way, how I would handle the labor pains and what the birthing process would be like. Benny and I attended Lamaze classes, but the experience just didn't seem reassuring enough. Underneath all of my wonder and self doubt, I truly believed I was ready to take on the challenge of being a young mom.

That day as I was waiting for Benny to show up, I felt a gush of warm water running down the inside of my legs. I remembered from the Lamaze classes that more than likely my water had broken, signifying the onset of labor. In an instant reality settled in, I was going to have a BABY! I started to panic and cried as fear of the unknown set in.

Momma's response was, "You should've thought of that before you got pregnant. You made your bed and now you must lie in it."

Despite Momma's acceptance of my decision to carry through with my pregnancy, she was still quite disappointed with me.

Benny arrived to the house thinking he was coming to pick me up to hang out and quickly learned our baby was on the way. Momma rode down to the hospital with us and I was admitted into Labor & Delivery and provided with a gown to slip on. After slipping into the hospital gown, the nurse confirmed that my water had broken and advised me to walk around outside of the room to trigger my contractions.

At that point, I felt no pain and believed the process was going to be easy after all. I had wasted so much of my time worrying and it wasn't even that bad, but within an hour of being admitted, I began to feel the pain from the contractions. They started off as bad cramps that grew progressively worse. I ended up having to lie down as the pain increased.

At some point, while I was lying in the delivery bed, momma told me she was leaving so she could get my little brother, Jeris in bed and ready for school the next morning. I felt completely crushed because I so badly wanted her to be a part of the process. What would I do without my mother next to my bedside? I was so saddened that momma seemed to have no intention of being there for me, to support me through such a traumatic experience. She'd given birth three times and I had no idea what to expect with the actual delivery. I really desired to have momma by my side to help me through this new and very scary experience.

After momma left, my labor pains became intense. I turned down every bit of pain medication the nurse offered me, though. I was determined to protect my baby from any side effects that could come from any medication they might give me. I believed I had to be strong and tough it out, so that's what I did.

During the 1970's there was a popular movie out called *The Exorcist*. In it, actress Linda Blair played the role of Regan, the possessed child. While I wasn't possessed with any form of a demonic spirit, I looked as if I was. Much like Linda Blair's character in the movie, with each contraction I would writhe around with massive and uncontrollable convulsions.

Benny tried to help but he had forgotten everything we learned in our Lamaze classes, so the times that my contractions hit its peak, he would lean over me and instead of guiding me through the breathing exercises in the manner that we were taught, he would sternly demand for me to "Take the pain" and at one point, I yelled back at him, "You take the pain," but that was completely useless.

Five hours after my water broke, Benny and I became the proud parents of a tiny little, premature baby boy that would change our lives forever.

One part of the birthing process that I still regret 'til this day was not accepting the offer to be the first to hold my baby boy that I had pushed out into this world. Prior to my delivery, I heard of another young mom refusing to hold her baby immediately after giving birth, which I allowed to influence my decision to hold my little blessing. My decision to survive my delivery without taking any medication had caused me to feel completely exhausted, so my only desire at that time was to have an extra moment of rest and as a result, Benny was the first to hold our baby. But within a few minutes, Benny passed baby CJ to me.

As soon as baby CJ was placed in my arms, I knew we were bonded for life. He was born a preemie and the tiniest, sweetest little blessing that a mother could be blessed with. What a beautiful child we had brought into the world. I could not believe that I was a parent. This little soul gave me complete strength and a new path to follow.

My new mission in raising CJ was to strive at becoming the best mom I could possibly be. Although the birth of my child was extremely traumatic for me, this was the little precious soul that caused me to fall in love with becoming a parent.

CJ was so helpless and had to rely primarily on me and Benny to provide him with the love and care he deserved, in order to survive in this huge world. This was a new life; a part of me and a part of his father that had been created out of pure love. This was so unlike how momma said I had come about - the result of a one night stand. Being blessed with the life of my little precious soul brought me complete happiness and provided me with an amazing drive to succeed, with a great purpose. CJ's success in life depended greatly on the decisions I would make in the years to come.

A few days following CJ's birth I was informed that CJ would need to undergo extensive testing for a suspected blood disorder that could possibly limit his life span. The medical staff conducted multiple blood tests on him and continued to get the same results. The medical team of doctors at the hospital didn't relay much to me during my stay in the hospital and instead, advised me to follow-up with his pediatrician for further testing.

When I took CJ in for his initial checkup with the pediatrician, the nurse informed me that additional testing was necessary. At that time, I began to assert myself by asking questions to learn more about the tests they were planning to perform. I was aware that the matter was serious, but uncertain how serious this suspected condition was.

I was instructed to take CJ to the lab area where blood tests were conducted. They had to prick CJ's heel as they had already done multiple times during his hospital stay. It was at that time that I inquired about the risks CJ was facing with the suspected blood disorder. It was then that the nurse relayed to me that a problem with CJ's white blood cells could possibly end his life before he turned two years old. That is when my heart to sank. I could not believe what I was hearing and felt as though I was being punished for becoming pregnant at such an early age in my life. I had sacrificed so much to keep my baby and was now facing this devastating news. CJ had brought so much joy to my world already. I needed to do whatever was necessary to preserve the life of my new baby. I knew I would not be able to survive without him.

I was now living a new life that was steering me in a new direction as a young mom of a child who needed me. I had spent my entire pregnancy praying for my little blessing to make it into the world and now I found myself praying for my baby to be healed from this suspected blood disorder that was threatening to claim his life. All I had during this struggling time was my faith and belief that all would turn out fine.

After praying for many days and nights, the test results came back. I was informed by the nurse that CJ would be fine. The results indicated that there were no further concerns regarding his ability to ward off infections. After receiving this wonderful news Benny and I moved forward in planning out our future together. Benny enlisted in the military and was sent off to the East Coast to complete basic training. I was still living with my mother at the time and babysitting another baby just three weeks older than CJ to earn some money.

The lady I was babysitting for was also a single mother and could only afford to pay me $50.00 per week. Of course I was satisfied with it, but it wasn't good enough for my mother who told me I would have to move out on my own because she could not afford to support me and CJ. I didn't know it at the time but she and my sister Shereese had submitted an application for me to move into an apartment complex specifically for single parents.

When I found out what they'd done, once again, I was faced with feelings of rejection by my mom. I was being forced out from under my momma's roof and into a program with complete strangers. There was very little for me to say or do that would convince my mother to allow me the stay in her home.

Although I silently questioned how my mother could send her daughter and tiny grandbaby away, I always understood that momma wanted me to learn how to survive on my own. Through her spirit of tough love, she followed her heart in doing what she believed was best for me and that was forcing me to get a taste of the "real world." I had no one else to lean on for support, so my only option was to follow through with the move into the single parent housing program.

CJ was six months old when we moved out of my mother's house. Leading up to that time, CJ cried a lot and didn't do well when others attempted to hold him. But, when we moved out, I noticed that CJ displayed much more happiness and that is when I realized it was the best move I had made as a new parent.

After moving into my apartment, my father picked me up to take me furniture shopping. He explained to me that he was only planning to cosign for me and I would be responsible to make the required payments, which would assist me in establishing my own credit. At that time, I was surviving off of governmental assistance with a grand monthly total of $280.00 per month, in addition to food stamps.

Adding the furniture bill to my list of expenses was a crash course in my ability to learn budgeting and also how to stretch a dollar around the block. I still had rent to pay, diapers to purchase and various small bills, like phone service and utilities. There certainly was no money to have fun with.

After moving in, I learned it was a requirement of each tenant in the program to attend monthly meetings with their assigned counselor and my counselor's name was Macy. She welcomed me into the complex, then promptly scheduled our first appointment.

Macy was more like a career coach. During our initial meeting she informed me about the expectations and requirements of the housing program, then asked me what my future goals were since the housing program had a two year housing limit. At the end of that two year period, I was expected of me to fully transition into more of an independent lifestyle. I had no idea what my goals were because I had never given "goals" much thought. Although, I did feel that moving into my first apartment was a great goal that I'd accomplished, I had no idea where I was headed after that.

My earlier plans to attend college had been shot down by my high school counselor as a result of my low GPA, so I did not know how to answer Macy's questions. At that time, I felt I had reached the peak of my success. I was a mom and now had my very first apartment. What more did I need?

Macy told me that her job was to guide me for the next two years so I could become more self-sufficient. That meant finding a job, enrolling in school and participating in three required courses offered through the housing program each month. In addition to all of that, I was expected to utilize the onsite childcare for CJ. I was so protective of CJ that up to that point, I had refused to allow anyone else to take care of him.

So, on top of everything else, this was the first dilemma I encountered. I needed to protect my baby and protecting him meant not placing him in the hands of strangers. I was left to figure out a plan as to how this was going to work. I had made up my mind that something would have to give and it sure didn't involve me sacrificing my son's well being.

During my meeting with Macy, she proposed two options. One option was for me to enroll in an associate degree program at a community college and the other option was a technical skills program. Since I had a two-year limit, I selected a technical skills program that would provide me with the tools needed to enhance my typing and computer skills, which was a six-month program. I relented on putting CJ into childcare. I realized there would be no real way for me to attend class without established childcare.

Having to enroll CJ in the daycare program was difficult for both of us because I was nursing him and he refused to take a bottle, so when I was in class, which happened to be located right above the daycare CJ was enrolled in, I could hear CJ screaming nonstop while being pushed along in his stroller or held and walked around outside by one of the daycare workers. This certainly stirred up my emotions because I desired so badly to be with my son. My instructor knew how difficult this was for me and made every attempt to comfort me by gently rubbing my back as she walked by while teaching. It was her effort made in assuring me that my child was fine. I wished so badly that I could leave class to console CJ, but knew that was not an option.

As difficult as it was for me to separate from my son, I knew it was only temporary. I reminded myself constantly that I had to do what was necessary in order to provide CJ with a brighter future. I pushed through the training classes despite feeling the agony of hearing him scream and cry for his mommy. CJ's crying lasted for weeks before he finally adjusted. The daycare workers were amazingly patient and diligent with him. It was under their care that my son finally learned to take juice from a bottle.

I had reached the end of the program and had experienced my first successful accomplishment as a single parent. I graduated from the program with my certificate and landed a job right away as a receptionist at a well known bank. The most exciting part about me landing employment was knowing I had the ability to cut my ties with welfare and the other governmental assistance that I'd come to rely on for survival.

In my new job as a receptionist, I was responsible for answering the phones and serving as the primary contact for the customers who entered the bank. There was one specific group of customers who attracted my attention the most and they were young college students who frequently came in to request information and applications for student loans to cover the cost of their education and housing. Every time a group of college students, who were all around my age, approached me to inquire about student loan packets, it increased my desires to attend college.

I appreciated the fact that I had landed a decent job, but I realized I wasn't satisfied. I worked in a department with a group of older people I couldn't relate to, or bond with. The highlight of my day was meeting up with a couple of younger women who served as bank tellers that I had developed a bond with. Both of them loved their jobs as tellers and would often encourage me to apply for a position within their department, but after serving so many college students, I just knew I wanted more than what the bank could offer me at that time in my life. I had grown quite miserable because I felt I was missing out on a huge part of my life every day that I catered to college students while dreaming of attending college myself.

After realizing and accepting the fact that I strongly desired to enroll in college, I parted ways with the bank as a receptionist and arranged a meeting with Macy to inform her of my new plan to attend college to earn a four-year degree. Macy wasn't in favor of my idea and made every attempt to discourage me, reminding me that my housing program had a two-year limit and I only had a little more than a year left in the program. I assured Macy that I had a complete understanding about the challenges I would face, but had a made up mind that I would follow my dreams and accomplish my goal in applying to and enrolling in a four-year degree program.

I knew I would have to have a good plan established by the end of my two years in the housing program. I refused to allow myself to become discouraged and instead, held on to my faith and belief that everything would work itself out in the end. I had no intention of starting something I couldn't finish. Also, there was no way I was giving Macy the upper hand in dictating which direction my life would take, based on what *she* believed was best for me.

My very dear friend Yolanda, who I'd grown up with, had been encouraging me to enroll in college after witnessing so many of the struggles I had encountered during my early adolescent years. I had a lot of trust in Yolanda because she witnessed so many of my struggles and still remained quite close, always desiring to help me in any way possible. What was so special about Yolanda was the fact that she had a strong ambition to succeed in life. By adulthood, Yolanda, her sisters and I had grown to become so very close that although there was no blood relation we had become more like family. Their loyalty and friendship was so genuine, not once did they ever turn their backs on me, even during the times my decisions, behavior and drastic changes were quite questionable.

Yolanda had entered college straight out of high school. By the time I had made up my mind to attend, she was in her junior year and seemed to be breezing through. Of course, I turned to her for help to accomplish my enrollment goals. By the end of that August, I had successfully enrolled in college and was walking around the campus grounds living my life as a new college student.

Everything managed to fall into place with my new college experience, which assured me that the new path I was traveling was in the best interest of myself and young son. I already had CJ enrolled in the childcare program affiliated with the college campus, so my need for childcare never presented as a problem during my transition into this next phase of my life.

A few months into attending college, I realized just how big of a trial I had taken on. Throughout my high school career, I had developed extremely poor study habits, so establishing discipline at the college level was by far, my greatest challenge of all. What made it all the more so, was the fact that I was a young mom of a toddler, attempting to make a better life for the both of us.

My first year was devastating. I was facing academic suspension because my grades were terrible. I quickly learned that my pending suspension also locked down my ability to apply for financial aid. If I allowed them to fully suspend me without putting up a fight - a much healthier fight than what I'd engaged in during my younger days - I would not only fail myself, but also my son. He would lose out on a great childcare program with wonderful teachers and classmates that he had enjoyed for the past several months.

My son was relying on me to succeed, just the same as my siblings and I had to rely on our mother. Remembering the mistakes that my mother had made just made me more resolved to not put my son through the same. I refused to allow the financial aid office the opportunity to shut the door to the promising future I desired so badly for my son.

I waited in the long line to meet with a financial aid counselor and after meeting, was informed that the only option available to me was to write a letter of appeal and submit it to the Financial Aid Review Committee. Once reviewed, a decision would be made regarding my suspension. I took the paperwork that the financial aid representative provided me with and worked on writing my appeal that night. I submitted all the paperwork to the financial aid office prior to my assigned deadline and anxiously awaited their decision. Unfortunately, my appeal was denied.

Devastated and desperate, I went right back to the financial aid office. There had to be other options. I was not ready for my future dreams to end up shattered. I knew it was imperative for me to do everything in my willpower to remain in school. The financial aid counselor informed me that if I didn't agree with the process, I had one last opportunity to submit a second appeal and that is what I did. I wrote a very thorough and lengthy appeal. This appeal counted the most and would ultimately determine my fate. I put all that I had into writing my final appeal. I turned it in, then once again found myself anxiously waiting to learn of their decision.

By the start of the next fall semester, I still hadn't heard what the fate of my future college career was looking like. I had no funds to purchase my books and was on the brink of losing my childcare unless I proved that I was enrolled in school. If I lost out on my school benefits, that meant I would also lose my job I had earned through a grant-funded work study program. I was facing a significant financial loss if my second appeal was not approved.

Three weeks into the semester, I returned to the financial aid office and waited in the long line to inquire about my appeal status. This time the news was just what I needed to hear. My second appeal had been approved. I had basically begged them to allow me a second opportunity to prove myself and assured the Financial Aid Review Committee that I would never again end up in that type of predicament. I had gone so far as to promising them that I would graduate with an above average GPA if they allowed me to continue my studies. On a side note, I went on to do just that!

After learning that my second appeal was approved, I dived into my school work. Although I had fallen behind, I was able to catch up with all of the assigned classwork in all of my classes and worked hard at improving my grades by constantly monitoring my GPA to prevent it from slipping too low.

During that time, I reached the end of my term in the housing program. My two-year limit had come to an end and I was forced to move in the middle of the semester of my second year in college. It was tough, but I managed to establish housing and maintain a decent GPA throughout. It took me four and a half years, but I did it - I graduated with a GPA above a 3.0 and was awarded a TRIO Achiever Award for successfully overcoming the many obstacles I had faced during college. After receiving that award, I was nominated for a regional district award and flown out of state to give an acceptance speech. It was my very first speaking engagement in the presence of a large audience. After the closing of my speech, I received a standing ovation before receiving a beautiful plaque, awarded to me by the nominating committee. I felt completely honored as an ASPIRE recipient and the experience validated the self worth of my *good* fight in life. Throughout my college years, I had learned to fight in a much healthier manner for the desires of my heart and was now reaping the benefits of what I grew to accept as the good fight of faith.

I kept my promise to myself and the Financial Aid Review Committee. They were never provided with another opportunity to suspend me. It was a great feeling – I had proven to myself, Macy and anyone else who had doubted my ability to successfully complete my four-year degree that they were wrong.

Although my years in college were extremely rough, I never experienced any regrets or allowed any of those challenges to stop me from acquiring my degree. In making my decision to keep my baby, I'd also decided to come out of the darkness of my past. Wanting to make a better life for my son ignited a strong drive and will inside of me to succeed. I taught myself that I could do anything that I put my mind to.

I earned a bachelor's degree in Human Services. I had gone into that field with a strong mission to assist kids who were experiencing many of the same or similar circumstances I had experienced in life. Young people who were considered "at risk". How proud I felt and what a reward it was to have earned the ability to give back to my community.

Having this degree meant I would no longer have to depend on the welfare system for assistance. Having to wait for my monthly $280.00 check to support myself and son would soon fade to nothing but a memory. I was anxious to locate employment that offered decent health insurance and desired to experience purchasing food without having to tear food stamps out of a little booklet.

I landed my first post-graduate job as a counselor working with homeless and runaway youth, which primarily included teen prostitutes, gang members and mentally challenged teens. The pay wasn't great, but I had finally attained health coverage for myself and CJ through my job. An additional asset to the job I'd landed was through a loan forgiveness program that allowed me the opportunity to work off my student loan debt for time served in the field as a professional. A tremendous benefit because I didn't have to deduct funds from my salary to cover the additional burden of student loan payments. My income was already stretched thin trying to cover all the expenses that came with having a small child - keeping CJ fed, clothed and enrolled in before and after school care was amazingly expensive.

After two years of working and struggling to survive on a limited salary, I knew the only way to advance in my career would be to return to school to earn a master's degree. I definitely needed to earn more money. CJ had developed asthma during my early college years which contributed to plenty of medical health expenses as a result.

Having to return to school was an extremely sad moment and I felt so bad for CJ because I had already put him through so much, having to leave him at daycare from open to close while working long hours. Thankfully, the campus daycare where CJ was enrolled operated between the hours of 6:30 a.m. and 10:00 p.m., to accommodate the parents and staff who attended or taught late evening classes. There were a couple of semesters that CJ had to remain at daycare from sun up to sun down, depending on my class and work schedule and I hated having to leave him for so many hours each day, but again, I knew it was only temporary. It would take me two years to earn my master's. After that I vowed I'd find a job that left room for us to spend quality time together, every day.

I explained to CJ what was going to happen and that he only had to deal with this insane schedule for another two years. It was hard on both of us, but I had to do what was necessary for our continued survival. I had to turn to Benny's family for a great deal of the support in striving to successfully accomplish my goal. I just had the challenging task of **Learning to Forgive.**

12

Learning to Forgive

"I want you all to write an autobiography of your life", was the request made by Dr. Brenner during my undergraduate studies. "In order to go out and help others, you all will have to deal with your own stuff... there is a reason why each member in this class has a desire to go out and help others."

Everyone got quiet and my thoughts started racing as I stared at Dr. Brenner. My initial opinion of the assignment was that Dr. Brenner just desired to read our business and be nosey. I wondered if Dr. Brenner really expected me to share my life's history with him. After years of my mother teaching me to keep my personal business to myself, this assignment seemed ridiculous. Dr. Brenner continued to provide us with information about the assignment and explain his expectations of what he considered as quality work and I realized a huge portion of my final grade weighed heavily on how honest I was willing to be.

A few weeks later, I was approaching completion of the assignment and it was the first time in my life that I'd released my pain through writing and learned about myself. Having to complete that assignment taught me to perceive life in a different light and also taught me about the value of forgiveness. Writing this autobiography was the first time in my life that I learned to openly share information about my personal experience and many of the challenges I had encountered in life. I also learned to appreciate Dr. Brenner, while being thankful that he was the only one I was sharing my personal story with.

Writing the paper about my life was not an easy task to get through. After developing an understanding of Dr. Brenner's reasoning, I realized it all made sense and that it was important for me to make healthy sacrifices like this. It was necessary for me to work through my pain as I strived towards accomplishing my goal in earning my degree.

The day I turned in my paper was the day I handed over my heart and soul. On that day, I realized how much baggage I was holding onto and also learned that I was holding myself back from completely growing. I learned that I was blaming many of my unhealthy actions and angry behaviors on Hades and the abuse he had inflicted upon me. I also blamed my mother for allowing this evil man into our lives and then telling me years later that she should have remained with him and allowed him to continue beating my ass, in response to my behavioral issues and the trouble that followed. Those words struck me hard because I felt she failed to understand how much pain Hades had caused me. Pain which contributed to many of my unhealthy actions and angry behaviors.

After completing the required writing assignment, I learned that I was the only one responsible for the path I chose to travel down, regardless of what had happened to me in my past. I just had the challenging job of owning up to and accepting responsibility for my own actions and behaviors.

As much as I wanted to blame Hades and eventually, many others for what they had done to me, I realized the only one I could continue blaming for my actions and behavior at the end of the day, was myself. I had to learn how to take full control of my actions and also learn how to appropriately respond to difficult situations. So often, I felt as though I had been cheated in life, dealt a bad hand of cards, but realized I could not continue playing the "victim" role. In doing so, I was giving my power away. It was imperative for me to begin taking steps towards forgiving others, in order to flourish mentally and emotionally.

Another challenge I faced was learning to forgive Benny for allowing our relationship to be torn apart. He'd gone on to start a relationship with another woman named Nia, who soon gave birth to their baby girl. They'd named her Dahlia, the name I'd selected during my pregnancy, if we were to have a daughter. Learning to forgive Benny over the birth of his baby girl turned out to be easier than I ever imagined it would be.

It was Christmas Eve and I'd arrived at Benny's mother's home to drop CJ off so he could celebrate Christmas with his father's side of the family. When I entered the house I noticed Benny, his girlfriend, and their newborn baby girl. My heart sank. I ached all over from the pain of their new baby because I knew deep down in my heart that my relationship with Benny had ended for good. There was absolutely no way I was going to knowingly place myself in a position to become a second-hand woman to any man, especially with another "Baby momma" involved.

We had already been through so much as a young couple trying to survive the test of time, so I knew I had to build up the strength to move on with my life, to avoid becoming caught up in a love triangle. I had dreams of having all of my children by the same man, but our bond was broken for good and my trust completely shattered.

While trying to gather my thoughts and feelings, Benny's sister, Georgia approached me with Dahlia cradled in her arms and asked me if I wanted to see the baby. Inside, I was screaming in agony and couldn't believe Georgia had approached me with this baby that I had absolutely no interest in seeing. I was hurt and my wounds were so deep, but there she was, standing right in front of me.

Before I could respond, Georgia handed Dahlia to me all swaddled up and all I could see was her beautiful little face at just three days old. My first thought was, "What in the hell are you doing?" The room had grown completely silent and I'm sure I wasn't the only one asking that question.

After placing Dahlia in my arms, it was almost immediately that I fell in love. Every single ounce of love I had for Benny seemed to transfer right into baby Dahlia. She was so precious, helpless and innocent. I just couldn't continue to remain hurt and upset. This precious soul was a gift from God and even though she had another mother, she was still CJ's baby sister, so I learned to suck up my feelings. That was one of the first steps I had taken in learning to forgive, accepting the fact that this tiny little soul had not asked to be placed in the predicament she was born into. I made up my mind that for the sake of CJ having a relationship with his new baby sister, I would have to let go of the animosity I was feeling towards Benny, so that is what I did.

By the time Dahlia was three months old, Nia and I had grown close and shared the same desire in raising our children together. We wanted to support and build a strong sibling bond between our children. CJ and Dahlia were born into this world as brother and sister and it was up to us as the adults to keep their bond as strong as possible.

Nia and I arranged a time with a professional photographer to have their first sibling pictures taken together and as they grew older, Nia and Benny would often call on me to watch Dahlia for them whenever they wanted to have a date night, or were scheduled to work late and I gladly accepted.

Even though my relationship with Benny hadn't succeeded, I had strong hopes that he and Nia would remain together as a new, young family.

I grew to accept and treat Dahlia as if she were own. I was still single at the time, but it didn't stop the close relationship the three of us were able to develop after Dahlia's birth. Benny, Nia and I had all become friends and were so cool that whenever they would arrive to drop Dahlia off, we'd sometimes sit around and talk, or play silly games while CJ and Dahlia watched.

The special times that I was given the opportunity to model tender loving care towards Dahlia warmed my heart and I felt so pleased to have the ability to play such a huge role in her life and serve as a second mommy. When I finally did get married, Dahlia served as our flower girl, one day prior to celebrating her fifth birthday. CJ was the ring bearer and I wouldn't have had it any other way. All of this was made possible by my ability to surrender and forgive.

As a result of learning to forgive, I noticed that many of the challenges of life had become so much easier to get through. I could no longer stand to burden myself with the undesired pain that I held onto for so long. I had grown to realize that life was just too short and precious to waste time holding on to grudges. Through learning to forgive, I had also grown to understand spirituality at a much deeper level, an understanding that would lead me to step **Into the** path of **Light** during my spiritual journey.

13

Into the Light

Goal setting had become the norm for me and I continued to prosper in developing a strong drive to succeed in life. I was slowly transforming into a new person and realized the struggle I had fought so hard to overcome had finally paid off in so many positive ways. I continued to battle against defeat and experienced a period in my life where the dreadful word "No", was not an option I was willing to accept. I desired to make the unthinkable happen in my life and was willing to go the extra mile to attain my goals, even if it took a little longer to reach.

After enrolling in graduate school, I explored the idea of purchasing property so I could raise my son in a much safer environment. I continued to fight the good fight in making every effort to prevent CJ from experiencing anything similar to the life I was exposed to as a child. So establishing stability for him had become my top priority.

I started off by visiting multiple financial institutions to inquire about the application process for a home loan. I was a young single mother with debt, surviving off of a limited income and residing in low-income housing at the time, so I was turned away by many, but every time I was turned down I developed a fire inside to continue pressing on to make my dream of purchasing property become a reality, with the faith that I would eventually be approved. I continued to pound the pavement and even took my step to another level, driving around with CJ on weekends to visit with real estate agents who were hosting open house visits for property listed on the market. I asked a lot of questions and gained enough information to know what was necessary for me to accomplish my goal.

Through my own research, I learned about a few federal programs that were offering funding to first time home buyers. I contacted a few of the agencies to inquire about what steps were necessary in order for me to qualify for a home loan. The initial challenge I had in qualifying for the loan program was paying off my outstanding credit card debt. Gwen, the loan officer pulled my credit report and as she reviewed it, she outlined the debt I needed to pay off in order to qualify for the home loan program. I followed Gwen's advice with the strong mission to purchase my first home, refusing to allow any obstacles to get in my way of successfully accomplishing my new personal goal.

I had finally reached the point of paying off all of my debt with the income I was earning from my full-time job as a family advocate for a nonprofit agency and also from my part time job as a youth tracker, monitoring youth committed by the District Court to the custody of the Division of Youth Services. As a family advocate, I always went the extra mile to assist the families assigned to my caseload to the best of my ability and now it was time for me to help my own family. After paying off all of my debt, the time had come for me to move forward with the process of applying for my home loan. I was approved and blessed to finally reach the date of closing on my property, a few days prior to my birthday.

A month after I closed and had become settled into my new home, I was contacted by a journalist of a major local newspaper who told me that someone had anonymously contacted their office to report my success story. The journalist asked me if I would be willing to allow her to interview me for an article she was interested in publishing in the newspaper. I was initially hesitant and didn't really care to attract all of the undesired attention. I turned to Katrina, the director of the family center where I was employed full time, for advice. In addition to serving as our director, Katrina also fulfilled the role of a "mentor" in my life at that time. Katrina was a very well-known and respected social worker in the City of Denver and served as a professor at Denver University and the Community College of Aurora. I really looked up to Katrina and respected her because her heart was truly in the right place in reaching far beyond to help others in need. She always used a genuine approach in working with some of the most difficult people, so if I was going to ask anyone for advice, it would be her.

Katrina persuaded me to move forward with the article, telling me how many people I would be able to help by allowing my story to run. Katrina also reminded me that my story was positive compared to the amount of negativity that was often covered in the media.

The only one who was against me sharing my story was my mother, who always seemed to have a fear of embracing success. Here was yet another situation in my life where I had to make my own decision and live with it, even if it meant going against my mother's wishes.

I purposely didn't share it with my father because I knew his pride would prompt him to share my story with everyone in the family and I just didn't want to deal with that. After becoming a parent, I experienced a period of isolation from most of the members of my family on both my mother and father's side, so I had no desire to have my story shared amongst family members who I felt couldn't care less about my accomplishments. I hadn't even shared the plan with some of my closest friends. I just desired for the article to run quickly, so I could get on with my life.

I returned the call to the journalist and we arranged a time to meet. She also arranged a time for a photographer to stop by my new home. It was another time in my life that I had to release all of my fears and go with the flow of the light that I had longed to live in for so many years. I had a chance to be that glimmer of light for others who were facing darkness in their lives. Sharing my story would serve as an encouragement to others to prosper by chasing their dreams.

My mother never said much to me regarding my decision to run the article and when my father found out, he became my greatest fan. Daddy was the first to call me early in the morning on the day that the article was published. I wasn't able to hide it from him for too long. He was so proud of me and told me he had purchased multiple copies of the paper, with the intent of clipping the article out from the newspapers to mail out to other family members.

I admit that after speaking with my father, I wasn't too happy about his plan on sharing the article with everyone, but grew to understand and appreciate him for his genuine love, support, happiness and pride he displayed for me and my accomplishments.

A short time after the article ran, I was contacted by a representative of a local television news station who expressed an interest in inviting me in to their station for an interview. I had no desire to bring any additional attention into my life. I had become severely overwhelmed by all of the attention up to that point had me severely overwhelmed. I was still pushing to get through graduate school and working one full-time and one part time job. My time was extremely limited and as a result, I declined the opportunity. I knew it was imperative for me to maintain a strong focus and refrain from becoming sidetracked, so my only desire at the time was to return to my normal, everyday lifestyle.

Even with all of the attention, I remained humbled in knowing that my decision to allow the article to run had helped others and that is what mattered the most to me. I had spent many years of my life reading the horrific stories about the murders of so many of my childhood friends who had lost their lives to violence and felt a sense of pride in knowing I had survived through the darkness that so many us as children and young adults had been surrounded by.

I never experienced any regrets regarding my decision to allow the article to run. In fact, it was one of the best decisions I had made, aside of selecting to carry on with my pregnancy and keep my child. I was proud to be part of a story that was shared in the light of a world that often contains so much negativity and darkness through the very sad and painful stories that are often shared by the media. My next step in life would be understanding **Relationships with a Deeper Meaning**.

14

Relationships with a Deeper Meaning

My ultimate dream during my college years was to locate employment at a state youth detention facility, in order to work with detained youth since it was a field I felt I knew best.

As I was approaching graduation, an opportunity arose for me to apply for a state position as a correctional officer at a youth detention facility. My desire for the position faded quickly after learning that it entailed working overnight hours, holidays and double shifts, as needed. The job paid well and most certainly would have covered all of my financial needs, but I knew I would have to sacrifice CJ's wellbeing if I committed more time working to serve detained youth than the valuable quality time that was necessary for me to spend with my own child. I had made a personal vow early on to do everything in my willpower to prevent CJ from becoming another statistic and falling prey to the streets of darkness, so I knew it was imperative that I set an example for my son in the best way possible, to prove to him how much his existence meant in my life meant to me.

The idea of raising a Black son as a young single mother and possibly sacrificing him to the streets never set well with me. I had witnessed far too much to sacrifice my own son to the streets over a paycheck, so I passed up the opportunity in an effort to save my child. I, instead sought out "family friendly" employment that also met my financial needs.

Through my very own personal experiences, I learned first-hand that many of the situations and predicaments the young children were encountering started from within the home. I knew all too well what it was like to be left at home without adequate supervision while my mother worked multiple jobs to support our family. I most certainly did not want to repeat that cycle in having to rely on others to raise my child, knowing he needed me the most.

A few weeks following my graduation, I located employment working as a youth counselor for a homeless and runaway shelter for youth. The pay wasn't great and the job in itself was challenging for me because I never imagined that I would become a witness to so many hurting youth who were carrying such heavy burdens in their young lives. I certainly had my share of problems growing up, but it definitely wasn't anything similar to what these youth were experiencing. These were children living on the streets with no place to turn.

So many children were suffering through their struggles in trying to find a clear path out of their own darkness. The experience certainly raised my awareness even more in knowing that I had selected the right profession to commit my future to.

One of the young teen girls had been gang raped and as a result, had been left with many invisible scars. Professionals in her home state where the violent attack occurred made arrangements for her to be transported to Colorado to escape the darkness she'd been surrounded by, in hopes of a better chance of survival.

Many other youth who took part in the program were affiliated with, or members of gangs and others were children who had either been kicked out of their homes, or had run away from home for any given reason.

The lives of many of the youth reminded me of a story momma would read to me about the little boy with the alcoholic father. A story that I had witnessed being played out in the precious life of one young soul in particular, that had come to the shelter for services.

During one of our regular staff meetings, another counselor relayed to our team that one of the boy's assigned to his caseload had disclosed to him that his father had kicked him out on the streets and would only allow him to return if he brought homeless or runaway boys back with him. His son would obey his father's requests, but sadly end up back out on the streets a night or two later. Ironically, if the boy's father took a liking to the boys he brought home, his father would allow them to remain but send his son back out in the streets. It was suspected that the father of the boy was engaging in sexual relations with the other boys, based on a lot of the information gathered, which turned out to be a matter that the director expressed his plans on addressing.

As line staff, we never received an update relating to the outcome of how things panned out for the father, son and the boys who were being lured into his home, but what we did notice was that the boy stopped coming in for shelter and services, so it was assumed that the matter had been turned over to authority.

I remained at that job for approximately one year before I was recruited for a daytime position at a detention center by a couple of the workshop trainers. The ladies introduced themselves as Sally and Jane and asked where I worked. After I shared my employment background with them, Jane asked me if I would be willing to join their team at a co-ed, maximum security youth detention center. I'd be their assistant, providing life skills training to the boys, during the scheduled shift of 7:00 a.m. and 3:00 p.m. My dream job had actually fallen into my lap and I was so happy. The only dilemma was, it was a six-month contract position with the possibility of turning into full-time employment. I knew it was a risk, but held on to my faith that all would turn out for the best. I saw this offer as an opportunity for me to get my foot in the door. It was definitely fitting to my requirement of not helping other children to the detriment of taking care of my son.

The time came for me to resign from my position at the youth shelter. One of my coworker's questioned my sudden move and told me that it didn't sound right, asking me if I was certain that I wanted to make that move. I loved my job and the population it served, but I felt I needed to take the risk, so I moved on with the confidence that all would work out for the best.

The new job started off great, with the exception of the distance I had to travel to make it for my 7:00 a.m. shift after dropping CJ off at before care. I was supposed to arrive by 6:50 a.m. to prep for my day. Unfortunately, the earliest I could drop CJ off was 6:30 a.m. and the travel to work during that time took at least thirty minutes to reach my destination. I knew I would be cutting it close, but still held on to faith that everything would work out.

I didn't know it at the time, but I was destined for failure with this "dream job" because the before care staff member was supposed to arrive to open the doors by 6:30 a.m., but never made it on time and instead, would roll up 10 to 15 minutes later each morning, constantly apologizing as she rushed to get out of her car. The delay in her arrival always caused me to get caught up in the early morning rush hour traffic, making it hard for me to arrive in a reasonable amount of time. That's when everything started going downhill.

Sally and Jane were initially understanding and allowed me to arrive 10 minutes past my scheduled shift, but even that wasn't enough time. I really desired to have this job, but the situation I was in prevented me from growing in my position. The before care worker's tardiness, combined with the early morning traffic and questionable weather in Colorado meant I didn't stand a chance.

The greatest disappointment involving this job, was when I asked for a review of my performance to see how I was doing, aside of my traveling and childcare issues. Other than those two issues, I put forth my very best effort in doing all that I possibly could to earn a full-time position at this detention center. As it turned out, I wasn't given a fair chance to prove myself to begin with and I was convinced that it had nothing to do with my arrival time, or even my childcare issue.

After a few times of asking Sally and Jane if there was anything I could work on to improve in my position, Jane, the lead of our team finally responded to my inquiry as we were preparing our afternoon lesson plan, stating, "What are you talking about? We only hired you because you are Black."

I was blown away at that moment and my heart hit the floor. I had resigned from a job that I actually enjoyed, in order to take a chance at becoming a full-time state employee and here I was, feeling certain that it was not going to happen after so bluntly being informed that I was only hired because of the color of my skin. Sally and Jane's only reason for hiring me was due to the fact that they had a quota to fill and what better way to do it, than to bring someone in on a 6-month 'temporary' term with no intentions of ever filling that position on a full-time basis.

After realizing the predicament I had placed myself in, I felt completely foolish for trying so hard to keep a job that seemed too good to be true. The bad part about it all was the fact that it really *was* too good to be true. I was so devastated that I went to the ladies restroom and cried my heart out. As tears were streaming down my face, I fell to my knees to pray, asking God to give me the strength and ability to carry on and also to guide my direction to prevent me from failing my son. I had worked so hard to overcome barriers in life and sacrificed so much to get through school. Here I was with a college degree, having a door slammed right in my face.

As I approached the end of my six-month term serving as an assistant in the detention center, I was contacted by, Dr. Walstein, the director of our program. He called me into his office and asked me if I had another job lined up, being that I was a single mother with no additional income. When I told him I didn't, he offered to keep me on the payroll system until I located a stable job. He then referred me to a woman named Amy. It just so happened that a job similar to the one I was working had opened up at another detention facility.

When I connected with Amy, I found out the location of the detention center was much closer for me to travel to and the hours were more flexible. Amy informed me that she arrived every morning at 8:00 a.m., but didn't expect me at that time, unless I desired to arrive that early. She offered me the flexibility of arriving at 8:30 a.m. or 9:00 a.m. with an end time of 4:00 p.m., which was so much easier for me. Amy turned out to be very sweet.

A few months later, I landed full-time employment as a Family Advocate, with a great healthcare package and good pay. After coming so close to being unemployed, I wanted to make certain that I was earning enough money to survive with my son and vowed that I would never take such a risk again, so I worked my full-time job; in addition to a part time job that I had picked up a few months prior. Both jobs allowed me the flexibility I needed to prioritize my responsibilities as a parent, so I could still be available for CJ.

It was this situation that prompted me to return to school for my master's degree. The experience of working at both detention centers really opened my eyes and provided me with a sense of direction. I had earned my Human Services degree, but it was broad and geared more towards psycho-therapeutic work. I knew I would have a better chance landing a job in corrections with a master's in Criminal Justice

I took the Graduate Record Examination (GRE) that was required to enter graduate school and completed the application for one of the major universities located in the city of Denver. I was accepted and enrolled by that following summer. I took action on climbing to higher ground, which I knew would entail **Embracing the Light**.

15

Embracing the Light

Throughout the early years of CJ's life, I had attempted to create fantasy love on two separate occasions with two men I'd known since childhood.

The first was a man named Davis. Davis had two brothers; his younger brother Talon, was 18 when he was shot and killed during a robbery and his older brother, Ramone was serving a lengthy prison sentence when he was stabbed to death by another inmate. Both of their deaths were extremely difficult for me to take in because I had shared a friendship with all three brothers when we were children.

I contacted one of my best friend's, Sandra to share the devastating news and we arranged a time to meet up to view Ramone's body together. I thought I would have the opportunity to see Davis, but later learned that Davis was also in prison and hadn't been permitted to attend his brother's funeral. I felt so bad for Davis because I knew the sweet side of all three brothers. So, when I unexpectedly ran into Davis a few years later, I felt the need to share with him that there was a purpose for his life and encouraged him to remain on track, despite the tragic death of both brothers.

I developed this fiery passion to assist Davis in beating the odds that were stacked against him. As time progressed, I helped him enroll in college and also assisted him with developing a successful path to freedom. But it wasn't long before Davis admitted to me that he had no desire to change. He had become accustomed to the lifestyle he had lived all of his life. Davis admitted to fearing success and stated it was due to his track record of failing so many times in life. Davis also expressed his fear in making a positive change because he believed "haters" would shoot and kill him for making the effort to change his life for the better. He once described his premonition of an automobile pulling up to a stop sign, alongside of the car he was driving and shooting him point blank in the head.

Davis would constantly tell me how proud he was of me for making such positive changes in my life and encouraged me to keep striving for success. He would tell me, "Just don't ever forget where you came from and do it for all of us from the neighborhood that didn't make it."

Davis's words pierced deep into my heart and soul. After realizing and accepting the fact that Davis had no desire to change his lifestyle, we made a mutual decision to part ways. I was saddened, but decided to carry on in my mission to succeed.

Ten years later, there was a news report about a man being shot to death by a law enforcement officer for failing to exit the automobile he was driving. According to the report, Davis had gotten into an argument with his girlfriend, grabbed the keys to her car and sped off. As he was driving he happened to pass a policeman that had clocked his speed, several miles over the speed limit. As a result, Davis was pursued by law enforcement, however, failed to yield to a complete stop.

When the officer finally caught up with Davis, he was sitting in his car in a residential area, near a stop sign. The officer blocked the automobile Davis was driving and got out with his gun pointed towards Davis. He ordered Davis to get out of the car and instead of doing so, Davis reportedly gunned the engine. That's when the officer made the decision to fire his gun. The officer sprayed the car with bullets and that's how Davis died. He'd predicted his own death, just not quite in the manner that he expected. It turned out that it wasn't the "haters" that took him out for choosing to live in the light. Davis was trapped in the darkness and struggled to find a clear path out.

The second false fantasy I attempted to bring about occurred when I located a longtime friend from my childhood named Maurice. We dated for a very short time and it was evident that Maurice had no desire to change his lifestyle and really didn't care much for my changed lifestyle.

Eventually Maurice told me that he desired to be with the old Dionne. He said it was hard to not see me as the 'boxer' I once was, which made it difficult for him to accept my decision to live in the light. We had no choice but to part ways as a result. Another heartbreak, but I knew I had come too far to let it all go for someone who chose not to accept me for the positive qualities I had adopted.

Shortly after that break up, I found myself turning to my friend, Desmond, for support. He worked at the same facility where I worked full-time. Over the course of working together, we had developed a strong friendship. I found that I could share anything with him and he was always honest with me whenever he felt I was taking too much of a risk. In fact, Desmond had been very direct in telling me that I was wasting my time trying to save Davis because he wasn't ready to make the changes that were necessary to escape the darkness he was surrounded by.

Being the true friend that he was, Desmond gained my trust through offering his honest opinions that often came to pass and our friendship continued to flourish, eventually leading to our long-term marriage. I had married my friend and it was one of the best decisions I made. Desmond always seemed so happy and his presence in my life actually brought me more happiness.

When I first met Desmond, he reminded me so much of the kids I had grown up around; primarily the biracial ones that were half Black and Hispanic. I had no idea Desmond was half Black and half White until he was questioned during a debate one of my coworker's was having about race. During the debate, she stated, "Come on Desmond, you're half White… you know what I'm talking about" and I couldn't believe my ears. I had grown to feel so comfortable with Desmond and assumed that I knew his ethnic background, when it was actually quite different. To learn he was half White was a bit of a shock and setback for me because it caused so many issues from my past to arise; many of them involving unhealthy beliefs that I desired to move separate from.

Deep down in my soul, I desired to grow past the issue of race and color. I just desired to be happy with a soulmate who really understood and cared for me. I've always believed that how we appear on the outside does not define who we truly are deep down inside and for once, I needed to follow my heart. Desmond had certainly won my heart by the way he carried himself and the desire he had to succeed in life.

What struck me most was the fact that Desmond could relate to everything I had experienced in my life and more, so I had no desire to see race as an issue. I was willing to explore and give life a chance with a deeper meaning. I had no further desire to live in a broken and divided world. Instead, I decided to shove my personal feelings about race aside and set out to be more open with acceptance.

After developing a stronger relationship with Desmond, I learned that his mother supported him with embracing his

Black race also instilled the importance of valuing his culture, without "sugar coating" anything. Desmond turned out to know more about the roots of his Black race than I had ever imagined and I was extremely impressed.

Desmond's mother provided him with the tools he needed to learn how to fight against all odds. She also taught him that he was just as important as anyone else in the world and I grew to admire Desmond's confidence the most.

When Desmond invited me out on a date, I was impressed at how well he treated and respected me, by his genuine personality. I never had to worry about him pushing himself on me, which caused my trust in him to increase.

Our friendship grew into a deep care for one another, but before I allowed Desmond into my heart, I turned to CJ for his approval. After my previous mistakes with relationships, CJ had grown extremely protective of me, making every attempt to guard me from the darkness that he saw in my selection of men. I felt it was only fair to include CJ and consider his opinion since my decisions were affecting both of us.

When I asked CJ to share how he felt about Desmond, he thankfully encouraged my courtship by giving his approval. CJ knew that Desmond cared for him as much as he cared for me. Desmond showed a love towards CJ that I'd only seen displayed by CJ's father, so I knew the move would be good.

Desmond was well aware of my lack of trust in others and the embedded scars I had from failed relationships, so he provided me with the space I desired and maintained a lot of patience throughout our courtship. I was extremely reluctant to even become seriously involved with anyone at that time, and overall had nearly given up mentally and emotionally on relationships. Desmond was also well aware of my attempt to save Davis and the rejection I encountered from Maurice, so I felt completely vulnerable.

Desmond proved his sincerity by remaining by my side and by the end of that year we'd both realized that we shared many of the same goals and desires in life, so seeing the two of us together as an "item" turned out to not be as difficult as I initially thought it would be.

After allowing my guard to come down during my courtship with Desmond, I found it to be very refreshing to settle down with a man who was stable, trustworthy and not afraid to commit. Desmond was very gentle, patient and kind and gave me the time I needed to make certain I was ready to embark on a united journey with him. My life finally felt complete after making the decision to commit my future to Desmond and we became engaged and agreed to become one in God's eyes. I had entered a life that allowed me to embrace the light.

But it wasn't going to be all sunshine and roses. After making the decision to commit to one another, Desmond started to witness my anger for the first time. I'd managed to suppress it as I focused on what was best for me and CJ. I had spent years learning to be self-sufficient to accomplish what I needed, without the mental, emotional, financial assistance, or physical existence of a man in my life. It would take becoming pregnant with my second child to bring my lack of trust in men and my latent anger bubbling up to the surface once again.

I realized my anger had been festering over the years because my trust level in men had become completely shattered, even during my attempt to ignore the issue. Learning that I was pregnant caused me to feel even more vulnerable than I had already felt, and in a sense, trapped. After receiving confirmation of my pregnancy, I was devastated because I was just months away from completing graduate school and felt as though my pregnancy was going to hinder my ability to graduate. It was the first time in our relationship that I exploded. Desmond looked at me in a puzzled manner and allowed me to express myself. He was still interested in moving forward, but wanted to make certain we did whatever was necessary to strengthen our relationship, especially in knowing that we now had a child on the way. I managed to regain focus with Desmond's support and understanding and graduated that following May, just three weeks after delivering our son, Carter.

Desmond did not have a problem with CJ's father being involved in his life and in fact, would openly invite and encourage Benny to come around as much as he desired. It was important to Desmond for the three of us to get along for CJ's sake. One night, after Benny and I started arguing, Desmond pulled us together, relaying to both of us that we were all in it together, as far as CJ was concerned. He explained to us that there was no reason for arguing and that it was imperative for the three of us to create as healthy of an environment for CJ as possible. I couldn't believe what was coming out of Desmond's mouth. That is when I realized how much he really cared about *all* of us, as a blended family.

Desmond and I exchanged our vows in one of the most beautiful churches I'd ever been in. Desmond and I worked on the same campus where both of our jobs were located and as friends, we'd spend our breaks together, circling the building as we talked about any and everything imaginable. In that same building was a church located right across from my office. I always admired the beauty and elegance of the church. The inside of the church had cherry oak wood ceilings, which certainly complimented its serene appearance.

As Desmond and I strolled around the building during our breaks, he would listen to me complain about my failed relationships and other matters. Neither of us knew we were circling the building of the church that we would end up standing at the alter in, preparing to exchange our vows with one another. We had planned for our wedding to occur the following year, but after receiving confirmation of my pregnancy, moved our wedding ceremony up to an earlier date later that year.

On the day of our wedding, I was in my sixth month of pregnancy with our son. I knew it would be a challenge in my attempt to complete graduate school as a newlywed couple with a new baby joining our family, but I had strong faith that all would work out, and it did.

This time though, regardless of the healing I had yet to do, I was determined to succeed. Desmond had all of the positive qualities that I desired in a man, so it wasn't difficult for me to work on trusting that he would provide the emotional and mental support I needed in order to succeed in my master's program, in our marriage, and as a parent to our children.

Quite similar to CJ's birth, I went into labor with my second child quite unexpectedly. We had just celebrated Easter Sunday with my in-laws and after returning home, I got right to work on completing my comprehensive exam, which was the final step in my preparation of graduation. It was late in the night and I was typing out my answers to the final exam questions when I felt that familiar gush of water trickle down the inside of my legs. I freaked out and began to cry. I could not believe the timing of my unanticipated delivery. According to my recorded due date, I still had three weeks left.

I was in tears because I did not want to have my graduation delayed for any reason. I needed to find a way to complete my exam in order to fully complete school and earn my master's degree. I had made it to the very end of my master's degree program and yet, in a position once again facing a potential delay in achieving my goal. I was having none of that though. The first thing I did after arriving to the hospital was place calls to both of my professors. I left messages on both lines to relay to them that my labor had begun much earlier than expected. My professors had already suspected that I would deliver prior to their prescheduled exam date and for that reason, approved for me to complete it a few weeks earlier. I was sobbing as I relayed to both on their answering services, that I had only completed three-fourths of my exam. I had a deadline to turn my exam in and wasn't quite sure how it would work out.

I delivered my second son, Carter with few complications and was discharged from the hospital within a couple of days. I had barely been home for twenty-four hours when I found myself sitting back at my computer, working profusely to complete my exam. Little Carter was comfortably lying in my lap, nursing. My professors had approved the extension of my comprehensive exam by two days, since I had spent two days in the hospital.

I returned to school within days of leaving the hospital. I did not believe in presenting excuses. I knew what I had signed up for and was determined to complete it. I had a goal to complete and refused to allow any situation to interfere with my success. Not only did I turn in my completed exam on time, per my extended and approved deadline, but also completed all of the additional work assigned. I had successfully met the graduation requirements on time and proudly walked across the stage with both my sons and my new husband seated in the audience, cheering me on.

Although my stress level was high, I had made it and it was all well worth it. Once again, I had proven to myself that I could do anything I put my heart, soul and mind to and now I had an additional support system offered by my husband, who had managed to remain by my side since the very beginning of our relationship. Life most certainly felt much more stable than ever before.

I had learned to believe in myself even more as I continued to fight through life in a much healthier manner. I reflected on how I had learned to survive through so many of the struggles I had encountered as a single mother and how I had gained the confidence to stand on my own two feet for the sake of myself and my son. The only thing different was I now had a companion to help me with driving forward in a much positive lifestyle.

I had also fought hard to prevent my son from becoming a statistic in an environment where his future was not promised. I wanted better in life and knew I had to strive to reach all that my heart and soul desired. I was convinced that my life would have turned out much different had I allowed others to dictate which path my life would take. I was quite satisfied with the steps I had taken on my own, to reach my very own accomplishments with the assistance offered by others who believed in me and pushed me along the way towards the light.

There were many nights that I sat and cried happy tears because I had to learn how to survive the hard way, without the support I believed I deserved from my mother who, after considering to abort me, made the decision to bless me with such an abundant and rewarding life. But of course, those were my own feelings and beliefs. Momma had only desired the best for us and had a tough way of raising us as children, providing us with the tools to survive in the best way she knew how to.

It was up to me to take what I had gained from her teachings through her tough love, while striving hard to produce positive effects. I may not have been cradled through life by my mother in the way I desired, but I was spiritually carried in life by my Spiritual Father, quite like the poem "Footprints" by Margaret Fishback Powers.

Throughout my transition of experiencing a new life in the light, Desmond remained loyal in his commitment to marriage, which caused our relationship to strengthen each passing year of our marriage. Desmond and I were blessed to have a total of five children together, including CJ. Desmond had gained every bit of my trust through his genuine spirit. Sure, there were some rough moments throughout the years of our marriage, but we managed to hold the vows that we'd exchanged deep in our hearts and through much prayer, we survived many of the storms that threatened to ruin our union.

Patience turned out to be one of the most valuable lessons I had learned in life, which also assisted me a great deal in learning to appropriately channel my anger in an effective and much healthier manner. Desmond also displayed an enormous amount of patience towards me, and just having him involved in my life helped ease so much of the anger and pain that was so deeply rooted from within.

Over the years, I have learned to gain more self-control of my emotions and for that reason, my anger doesn't show as often as it did in the past. I am certainly not claiming to be perfect by any means therefore, and well aware that there will always be areas for me to work on and improve. With all that I had been through in my past, having the ability to expand in my growth meant **Learning to Love** more and accept what I knew I deserved in life.

16

Learning to Love

Momma tried her best to provide the best care for her family that she possibly could, but what is the true definition of family? While searching for my own meaning of what "family" meant, I found myself being drawn to certain types of families that displayed the love and affection I often felt deprived of.

After Shereese left home and returned many years later, she happened to mention to momma that we had a 'dysfunctional' family. I had never heard that terminology used before and therefore wasn't sure what Shereese meant, but after that word came up again during my early college years, I realized, gaining clear knowledge and understanding of the word was imperative for anyone expecting to earn their degree in Human Services. I was the next in line trying to explain to momma about our dysfunctional family lifestyle.

Every attempt we made to discuss our painful past with momma stirred up her emotions, causing her to become very agitated and offended because in her eyes, she'd done everything she possibly could to keep our family together and provide for us and now we were college graduates attempting to educate our mother, based on information we had learned during our preparation in setting out to help the world.

In order to create positive change in our lives, we had to see the bad in order to search for the good. To do so we had to learn how to identify the parts in our lives that were 'dysfunctional', then figure out how to separate from so many of those dysfunctional ways that negatively impacted our lives.

There were many cycles to be broken, but we first needed to recognize and accept the truth for what it was and momma just wasn't having it. She would rather have us throw that part of our "education" out of the door. There definitely was no plan for momma to rationalize about it and for that reason, that dreadful word was seldom brought up.

What I did learn to do was evaluate my past to figure out how to reach my desired future, by first searching for that family unification, love and happiness that so many other families seemed to display; the positive qualities of life I felt I deserved and should've experienced as a child, that I believed had been stripped away from me. There certainly was nothing loving or happy about being physically abused for failing to physically fight back with my peers if they were picking on me. A condition of treatment that nearly cost me my life on more than a few occasions.

There sure wasn't any love or happiness involved when Hades, in a position of trust and serving as an authority figure in my life, demanded that I pull out a chair to set in the center of the living room, for me to bend over so he could beat me with his belt. Not to mention the fact that

Hades would often cook crack-cocaine in our presence, then have the audacity to offer it to me at just eight years old. Or the embarrassing moment when he backed me up against the refrigerator with his nasty tongue hanging out towards my mouth, as if to kiss me. I just couldn't understand how momma could not see that as dysfunctional.

Momma wanted to bury her past and preferred that we focus on the fact that she got us out of the relationship, but the open wounds were still very present and unfortunately, had never been addressed in any way, shape or form. Momma didn't have to recognize it, but I sure as hell did and accepted the fact that in order for me to grow to my fullest potential, I needed to accept my past for what it was and strive to grow and create a brighter future.

As a child, life just didn't seem to be as happy and jolly for me as it seemed for many of the kids I watched on television. They seemed to have it all. I didn't realize, as a child, that it was all just an act they were putting on for the sake of producing a good "act". All I desired was to find the same happiness I saw in so many other faces. It was extremely difficult for me to find joy when my life seemed to be surrounded by sorrow, but as a growing child, I learned that true happiness must start from within.

After reaching my teen years, I still hadn't found the happiness I was searching so deep for. There just wasn't much for me to be happy about. In fact, so much of the darkness that I had experienced as a child was arising and starting to hit me in some of the worst ways, but I continued on with my exploration in trying to define my own true meaning of happiness. By my late teen years, I was finally able to branch out and search for the love and happiness I had missed out on as a child.

As I mentioned before, the first family that inspired me the most in identifying true love was the Gaines Family. No matter how hard life may have been for them at times, it sure wasn't evident because they always maintained a sense of contentment and also seemed to maintain a lot of peace through the storms. As siblings, regardless of those hard times, they remained strong in being there and supporting one another and also doing the same for their friends.

For anyone drawn to the Gaines Family, you would earn a friendship for life and that was a true treasure for me during the multiple storms I encountered after moving into my grandfather's property. It was through my relationship with the Gaines Family that I learned how closely bonded sibling relationships should be. A form of an emotional bond that I was never able to establish with my sister, Shereese.

Even though we grew up under the same roof, we were quite distant. I always desired to have a strong relationship with Shereese ever since I was small. I do remember being two or three years old and playing with my sister, as we rolled around on the floor. Shereese would give me a lot of hugs and kisses. I'm not sure what happened, but by the time I reached about six years old, the hugs, kisses and what felt like genuine love came to a halt and Shereese began to portray more of a hatred towards me. I would often confide in momma and ask her why Shereese didn't seem to like me much, but momma never seemed to have a direct answer until I was much older.

There was a time momma told me that Shereese was upset with momma for giving me more attention during my troubled years. Momma said she had tried to explain the situation to Shereese, but apparently momma's reasoning was never good enough. I don't know if Shereese ever understood the hell I experienced as a child, or whether she even cared to know.

All of that aside, I was destined to continue my search for that true love that really does exist within family relationships. I didn't want to settle for something that obviously wasn't meant to be, so whenever I crossed paths with other families that seemed to share that strong connection of love, value and support, I absorbed as much of it as I could.

During my later teen years after meeting Benny, I noticed a lot of love shown within their family too. In fact, the love they had for one another was quite unique and certainly something I didn't expect to ever see. Benny's parents were divorced. Each of them were in new relationships, yet they, along with their new significant others, spent many happy times together. In my tainted mind, I always witnessed animosity between couples who had broken up, so it was quite unusual for me to see a set of parents and their new companions playing cards, laughing and sharing good times together. It was through Benny's family that I learned the true value of forgiveness; a quality style of living that carried on and created a difference in my own life.

Desmond and I were able to develop a similar relationship with Benny. There were times when Benny would arrive to pick up CJ and end up hanging out with Desmond for a while, playing video games. After marrying Desmond, Benny's mother or sister would invite us over during special occasions, or just to hang out and that is when I realized how far I had grown with embracing family love and learning to model forgiveness in the same fashion as Benny's parents had, which brought more peace in my life.

By the time I reached my early 20's, I had developed friendships with so many others during my young adulthood who shared strong family bonds and seemed to have deep spiritual connections with their belief in the Lord. Those are the families I managed to cling to like a magnet, secretly adopting them while learning to adapt to what appeared to be much healthier lifestyles.

As a young mom, I shared a strong desire to grow more on a spiritual level which helped me establish a healthier lifestyle for my son. The emotional pain I had to deal with in having to learn to take care of myself, along with my new responsibility in nurturing, loving and caring for my own child was a lot for me to deal with. My only option the first time my life seemed to hit rock bottom for me, was to turn to the church I had grown up in for guidance, as an adult and young mom.

Early Sunday mornings, I would wake up, get myself and CJ dressed and walk nearly three miles to get to the church I attended when I was younger. I had fond memories of singing solos in the children's choir and thought it would be a good church for CJ to grow up attending. I would place CJ in his stroller and push him along for the 45-minute walk to church.

After arriving, I'd sit in the back area, most commonly referred to as the "Overflow" section, in case CJ made too much noise. CJ hadn't yet reached his first year of life and I was carrying a huge burden of confusion in trying to figure out the right path to travel, while learning to adjust to motherhood. I felt so alone after moving out on my own. At that time, Benny had joined the military to help provide for our son and he sure wasn't in favor of me living on my own with our child, but I didn't have a choice since momma made it clear that she could not afford to keep me and a new baby in her home, so the only option left for me was to strive for survival as best I could, while feeding my spirit through the Sunday sermons.

One particular Sunday, after locating a seat in the overflow area, the reverend of the church requested that the congregation stand to sing a few hymns. For some reason, I found my spirit to be moved in a way I hadn't felt before. I began to cry uncontrollably. It wasn't due to me feeling sad, but more of a reflection on my life as I silently thanked Jesus for keeping me through all of the struggles and hardships I had managed to survive.

As I continued to cry, one of the women in the church that I knew as a child approached me and embraced me with a hug, asking me what was wrong. I really had no way to respond to her question and understood that she was simply acting in good faith, with intentions of trying to help me. As I continued to cry, I began to wonder why her initial impression of me crying was perceived as though something was *wrong* with me. This was a Baptist church where emotions were not openly expressed often, so when she saw me crying, she seemed to assume the worst and attempted to intervene in the best way possible. I told her I was fine. It was just a moment of being in the spirit, feeling that pain and releasing it as my emotions flowed. I had reached a point of breaking down and knew that I needed God and would not make it in life without surrendering to Him. There was just no way for me to do it alone. I was now a mother of an infant son who would have to rely on me for many years to come. That was one of the first few moments I encountered in learning to strive towards more of a positive and responsible change in my life.

As I continued to progress in life and latch on to other families, my growth continued to flourish. I developed a friendship with a young man named Kyle, who I'd met at a church one Sunday. I was visiting my Aunt Norma who was a longtime member of the church. We'd lost contact with Aunt Norma for years after my Uncle Duke's tragic death and had recently reunited with her after learning she was heavily involved in church. I really loved my aunt and always admired her for her strength and the love she exhibited for Christ, so I developed a trust for the church she attended and would frequently visit there with my son. Sometimes I'd even attend with momma, my nephew and siblings.

This one particular day as I was leaving the church service with CJ, Kyle approached me as I was opening my car door for CJ to climb in. Kyle introduced himself and that was the start of our friendship. Kyle had a twin brother named Cole and a sister, named Melody. All three of them were kind natured people.

After developing a close relationship with all three siblings, I noticed the close-knit family bond they all shared which was very impressive to me. I also had the pleasure of developing a relationship with their mother, Ms. Grace, who was very strict, but also sweet and caring. I perceived Ms. Grace as a soldier for Christ, who was serious about her walk and seemed to only desire what was best for her children, as most mothers would.

Ms. Grace was my role model. I looked up to her and truly admired how well she had raised her children alone as she encouraged and supported them to remain close in what can often seem as a very harsh and cruel world. Although I thought the world of Ms. Grace, I didn't always feel as though she cared much for me. Sometimes I knew Ms. Grace did not like or approve of me much, but I was okay with that because I knew my heart and I also knew that I meant no harm. For so long, I had spent so much of my life attempting to prove to others that I was a genuinely kind person, even though I had the track record of making so many mistakes and all I desired was affirmation from Ms. Grace that she knew deep down inside of her heart that I was a good person.

Ms. Grace had raised very special children who were extremely talented. Kyle, Cole and Melody often traveled out of the country together to exercise their God-given talent in singing and during their travel, I would often stop by to check on Ms. Grace by paying her a visit, primarily because I cared very deeply for the family and truly valued their friendship as young Christian believers. The visits were very meaningful for me because Ms. Grace and I grew to know one another much better and I really grew to understand her.

When I was initially welcomed into the family, there were times she'd say very little to me, but I never really allowed it to get to me. What I desired the most and what made me happy was having the ability to absorb the love from such a spiritual, caring and close-knit family.

Through Ms. Grace, I learned to appreciate and value the sound of children laughing and playing together - a sound most would prefer not to hear - but Ms. Grace was altogether different. As she laid in her bed, she would close her eyes, as if to be taken over by the sweet sound of the play and laughter from the children outside of her bedroom window.

Even during the times I felt that Ms. Grace didn't care for me, I learned to cherish every moment of time we spent together. Ms. Grace taught me through her words of wisdom from a mother-to-mother standpoint and I was always very attentive. I knew she too, had experienced many hard times while raising her children and I also knew that Ms. Grace understood much of what I was going through.

Ms. Grace certainly was not one to bite her tongue if she felt the need to express herself, quite like the ways of my own mother. When Ms. Grace spoke, she often spoke with authority from deep within her heart and presented with pure honesty in relaying how she felt about certain matters, even if she knew it would be painful to hear.

On one of the days I arrived to check on Ms. Grace, she turned and glanced at me, then slowly looked away, as if to say, "Here it goes."

Ms. Grace was well aware that I was chasing love and when she opened her mouth to speak that day, I knew every word spoken was coming from deep within her soul. Ms. Grace basically advised me to focus on taking care of my son and her words hurt so bad because I had only arrived to keep her company and not to discuss my personal life. I was on a mission to find true love and really desired to be with a man of God, but the timing just wasn't right and Ms. Grace knew it and was brutally straight forward in letting me know.

As Ms. Grace continued to speak, her words penetrated so deep inside of my core. It was at that point, I felt certain that she didn't think much of me. I remained respectful and politely accepted everything she had to say, then went on about my life. Ms. Grace's words of wisdom never changed how I felt about her. I knew I would continue to be the kind and loving person I had always been deep down within, so I continued on with my journey.

It wasn't until after Ms. Grace's passing that I actually lived through many of the words she had left me with, realizing that she really did care about me. My three friends moved to another state to pursue their careers almost immediately following Ms. Grace's passing and I had experienced a major loss after their move. Many fond memories were created and I was left with treasures. Cole got married to his fiancée, Yvonne and CJ happened to be the ring bearer in their wedding. I was so happy for my friends, but also saddened in knowing that they were preparing to move on. I cried like a baby at their beautiful wedding. It was a step that I desired to experience so badly, but knew I needed to be patient and just wait for my big day to come around.

After my friends moved away, I continued to hold on to my relationship with Yvonne's parents, who I adored a great deal. It was rare for me to see a Black Christian married couple and I was so impressed with their relationship and the fact that they had raised two very beautiful and smart young women who they supported in moving on in their journey to explore life.

This was another family that I had secretly adopted and held onto very tight. Everything about this couple was absolutely beautiful. I always admired Yvonne's father who was proud to share his story of purchasing his dream car. Yvonne's parents also had a beautiful home in a peaceful neighborhood, much different than the neighborhood I had grown up in. I could not even begin to imagine how my life would have turned out, had I been blessed to live the life that Yvonne and her sister had lived, growing up with their strong and spiritually committed parents. What I did know, was I could certainly continue dreaming of a much brighter future until my own dreams came true.

My special friends who moved out of state left me with strength to carry on and also contributed to teaching me the value of family with the strong love that they all shared for one another, so Kyle, Cole, Yvonne and Melody and of course Yvonne's parents, and also to the late Ms. Grace, I sincerely thank you all for leaving me with an abundant amount of grace and love. You all proved to me that true kindness does exist and I really appreciate every single one of you for walking alongside of me throughout my learning phase and remaining sincere. A very special thanks to Melody for constantly reminding me that there was a purpose for my life. With everything I'd been through, I *really* needed to hear those exact words, which have remained with me ever since they were first spoken by you. I am so proud to relay that I have finally found my purpose and plan to continue persevering until I take my final breath.

As I blossomed into that young woman with the lifestyle that I always desired to have, I made it a common practice to absorb every ounce of love and support I came across. I absolutely cherished being around so many families where the love seemed to truly exist. Every single one of my experiences turned out as proof that through hope, prayer and living a much healthier lifestyle, the ability to find happiness and success was indeed possible. I also acquired the ability to experience much of what I always felt I had missed out on in growing up in such a darkened world, where it seemed to be more about survival.

Even though I came from a broken home, momma's passion and divine love for Christ left me with the knowledge and understanding that Christ is the light, which I have learned through my very own personal experiences.

One of the best treasures momma left behind was demonstrating her strength and ability to abruptly kick her addition to alcohol, cigarettes and unhealthy relationships. Momma was often misled by her thoughts and belief that turning to substance usage was a better way to cope with her pain, even if it caused her children emotional and mental harm. I know momma realized that she had allowed herself to become deceived in her belief that her only option was to accept the dark lifestyle she had learned to live in for so very long.

Momma put so much effort into learning to independently cope with the harsh reality of the pain that life so often dishes out. Momma was also one who learned to become a soldier for Christ with the love she shared through her belief and teachings, which definitely guided me into an environment where more genuine love from and for others was felt.

All of the love that I observed over the years left me with the ability to spread that same degree of love amongst my own family and our children happen to model that same quality of love and closeness towards one another that I witnessed from so many of my friends.

What I've learned is that strong family love can exist in any home, regardless of the socioeconomic status, or whether it is a one or two parent home. It is simply all about the decision one makes to remain in the light during the darkest of times. I know because I witnessed it with my own eyes and learned, when there is love in the home, there is also a strong sense of richness that no one can strip away unless family members become vulnerable and allow it.

Love has to be the seed planted as the foundation in the home because home is where it truly starts and that is where **My Spiritual Journey** initially began as a wife and mother.

17

My Spiritual Journey

So many of my very personal and traumatizing experiences as a child could have led me down an entirely different path. What truly saved me was learning to embrace spiritual growth and understanding for all that it was worth. I first had to accept the fact that life was never meant to be an easy slate for anyone. After growing up and believing that money bought true happiness, I realized that the lives of many individuals who seemed to have everything imaginable also experienced personal struggles of their own, which helped me to understand that happiness comes from within.

There were periods in my life that were downright depressing whenever I reflected on my past, but I learned to train my mind to understand that regardless of how sad or severe the mental, emotional and physical pain was that I had experienced, I had the ability to create a unique path through spiritual growth, in an effort to pave a much brighter future for myself. I just had to remain encouraged through my faith and believe that my life would improve.

It wasn't always easy for me to learn to believe strongly in the future that wasn't evident to me by plain sight, but I believed in dreaming of the better life I wanted and always felt I deserved. As I got older and started experiencing so many hard times as a young parent, I remembered the sense of community and support I had seen in the churches momma had taken us to. I found a church CJ and I could attend that fit our needs. As quick as I could, I joined the Bible study group. We attended as many of the potlucks that the members of the church put on. Being active in the church introduced me to many sweet and caring people.

One thing that stood out to me at this time was the fact that I only had Bibles that were gifted to me and not one that I had invested in on my own, so I decided to purchase my very first KJV Hebrew-Greek Key Study Bible and it turned out to be very helpful for me in understanding the Bible. My new Bible broke down scriptures in a way that was better understood.

That day is when I started reading the Bible for solace. I learned the scripture, "Faith without works is dead" (James 2:14-26 KJV) and that scripture is what inspired me to continue fighting in a good way for the treasures I desired to have in life. It gave me complete understanding that nothing I believed in, fantasized about or dreamt of, would come easy for me.

What lay before me now, was figuring out what steps I needed to take in order to follow my desired path to success. I wanted to get as far away as possible from that dark cloud I had been under for so long. Through strong belief and an amazing abundance of faith, I learned that the path I needed to follow was actually a very straight and narrow path and that meant, living a life of integrity in striving to do right in every way that I possibly could. As a growing believer, I always imagined that even if the human eyes weren't on me, God's eyes were. During my mission in learning to "Fight the good fight of faith", (1 Timothy 6:12 KJV), I learned to search for ways to beat the odds in my effort to overcome many of the discouraging moments that I was faced with.

At the age of seven, I spent many of nights praying for a little baby brother after momma shared with us that she was pregnant. After the birth of my brother Jeris, that is when I developed my first ounce of faith. As I continued to grow, I realized that many of my prayers had been answered, which definitely increased my faith. Every situation that occurred in my life had a very valuable lesson. I started to perceive my life as that of a puzzle slowly being put together and as I started to become more in tune with my spirituality, it hit me in accepting the fact that tomorrow is never promised and I would someday face a period of time in preparing to take my final breath of life.

In knowing and accepting the fact that I would one day transition from my physical existence, I had become that much more motivated to live my life in the most positive manner possible and to the very fullest. I also learned the importance of establishing and successfully accomplishing goals in my life, whether big or small and if some of those goals didn't pan out in a way that I expected, I'd explore other avenues to reach my desired destiny.

Until I developed more of an independence to read alone, momma spent a lot of time reading to me as a small child. There were some books that I learned to treasure the most. One of the story books was about the life of a little boy being raised by his alcoholic father. The little boy had a very loving spirit towards his father and seemed to have a strong desire to make his father proud of him, with hopes that his life would improve someday. One night, the father was upset after realizing he'd consumed all of his booze, so he sent the little boy out on the streets in the cold and wet rain to beg for money from strangers so his father could purchase more booze. While some rushed by, others stopped and dropped coins in the little boy's cup.

The little boy started shivering from the cold and wet weather, so he returned home with what money he was able to collect. After returning home, the little boy gave the money he had collected to his drunken father, who in turn, beat the little boy for failing to bring home the amount of money his father needed to feed his drunken habit. His father became so angry that night that he beat the little boy with a thick club and shoved him out of the house. The little boy walked and walked, with nowhere to turn and eventually found a large box to climb into. He fell asleep inside of the box, holding on tight to a little message a passerby handed him that read, *Somebody Loves You*. After the little boy fell into a deep sleep, the little message he was holding onto was carried away by the wind.

That book always comforted me during so many of the dark days I had experienced and it also instilled hope inside of me as a child. The book taught me that if that little boy could go through what he did and still be kind to others in the world, I could, as well. This is the life of many children who try so hard to please their parents and in turn, are mistreated by the very ones they should be able to trust. Unfortunately, this treatment could very well be due to substance abuse, holding onto bad feelings for an absent parent, or even due to the decision made by the parent to prioritize their need for another companion over their own kids, which contributes to their kids experiencing the struggle, while trying to find a way out of their own misery.

When my family expanded, I happened to come across that little book about the boy and shared it with all of my children and that is when I realized that the little boy had actually passed away at the end of the story. I suppose it was my yearning desire to see the glass as "half full" that prevented me from realizing that the child had died in the story. As a child, my initial perception of the boy climbing into the box was that it was his way of finding a way to escape all of the madness he had been subjected to by his drunken and abusive father.

I am convinced that had I realized the child had died during my younger years, I would have just held on to the belief that I was loved by *someone*, with the idea that there was little to no hope in a glorious and prosperous future, which I'm certain would've caused me to give up along the way, without putting forth a fight in so many ways for my survival.

Either way, I know and will always believe that the book reached my soul in the way it was intended, without thinking too deep about what had actually happened to the little boy. The book still means so much to me and I will always cherish and share it with my kids as a reminder to value the lives of children, especially as they grow older and experience challenges and hardship during their own efforts made in guiding the young precious souls of this earth.

As a growing child, I desired so strongly to search for and find what I believed to be true happiness. While the book about the little boy being abused and put out on the streets by his drunken father was more of a dark story, the message behind it has always been extremely powerful in validating the love by the unseen that we may not always feel on a physical level.

Many of us living in this world are exposed to various messages throughout our tender and precious years. Some of what we are exposed to will stick with us as a cherished experience and will hold great meaning in how we choose to live our lives. It is what is meant to be placed in our paths as stepping stones, where the greater challenge involved is just simply holding onto our faith. We all must continue to soar like eagles with the faith and belief that life will get better, while remembering that we are loved no matter what. In my very own effort to soar, I had to deal with one of the greatest challenges of facing the **Death of My Past** and making it a choice to put it to rest by forgiving myself for the situations I became entangled in and had no control to change.

18

Death of My Past

My life was full of highs and lows, but certainly more highs and what really mattered the most was how I chose to perceive many of those experiences. During my early college years, I learned a skill that provided me with the ability to view matters that occurred in my life more positively. The class demonstration involved a glass half filled with water and we were asked to share our perception of the glass as half full or half empty. The class was divided and while there was no correct answer, we all learned that day that the presentation was more about our perception and how we, as individuals chose to view life.

After being dismissed from class, I established a brand new outlook on life and began exploring alternative ways to view and tackle obstacles I had encountered. I also began to realize how much of an impact my internal perceptions had on my desired future.

As I learned to come to terms with my past, I searched for healthier ways to deal with so much of the hurt and pain I had living deep within my soul. I accepted the fact that I was carrying a load of baggage that needed to be released in order for me to continue growing and making effective, meaningful changes in my life. I had to find ways to release my anger, while learning to overcome the physical and emotional scars I had acquired along the way from so much of the violence that I was surrounded by. I struggled with having to face what I perceived as a demon that had haunted me early on in my life. By the time I reached this point in my life both of my parents were deceased. I no longer had the emotional, mental and spiritual support and guidance they'd provided me with.

My father passed away six years prior to momma's death. He was a man who I will always perceive as kind-hearted and generous. Daddy never really expected much in return for his kind gestures, other than the desire for others to maintain a loving and caring connection with him. While some fathers can be very harsh in their parenting styles, I can proudly report that daddy never physically, mentally or emotionally abused me. His way of physically disciplining me was to firmly squeeze my hand if I made any effort to try and wiggle my hand away from his and this typically occurred during times we were walking in crowded places, when he would make me hold his hand to keep me near.

Daddy was very generous in giving and would offer the shirt off of his back, as long as he knew he wasn't being taken advantage of. I expected nothing from my father, but his genuine love and support. Although I had been told on numerous occasions that he was not my real father, he was the only father I knew. He'd been in my life since birth, so in my eyes that made him my father and I refuse to see it any other way.

Daddy worked overnights for many years. Many nights I would act as his alarm clock by calling to make sure he was up and ready for work. These calls meant a lot to me. I would either play jokes on him or have deep conversations with him about life whenever he had a little extra time to talk. As I witnessed my father aging, I would have conversations with him about death, which was always difficult for me to fathom. Every now and again, I'd ask him if he was afraid to die and he'd reply so calmly with, "No, I am not afraid to die, it's a part of life."

One particular night, I had called to wake daddy up and after a short conversation, we disconnected and daddy left for work. He didn't make it though. Shortly into his commute, he had been on the highway when he whited out while behind the wheel. The car swerved and hit a guardrail, then flipped over onto its hood, before finally sliding to a stop. The condition of his car was horrific and the accident could've ended daddy's life, but he survived and I was grateful to God for sparing his life. Daddy had diabetes for much of my life. His crash was just one of many close calls he encountered with death during times that his sugar level would drop. Daddy never seemed phased by his condition or the danger it could put him in. Watching how he bounced back from the crash certainly put me at ease, but daddy was forced to take an earlier retirement, so his overnight position came to an end.

That sense of ease didn't help me much though because daddy was still struggling with his health-related issues. I remember he had a favorite chair in his kitchen where he would sit to take his insulin and every time I watched him insert the needle, my eyes would tear up and I'd walk out crying. Daddy never really knew how to respond about it, so whenever momma and I discussed it, she would tell me that the shots weren't painful to him. Her explanation was never enough for me because the pain still existed inside of me each time I watched daddy inject the insulin into his body.

Things would become even more difficult as his health deteriorated. Many of daddy's last days were spent being admitted into hospitals and transferred to various facilities. I visited daddy at most of the locations he was transferred to. Whenever I would arrive, daddy would always make a special appoint to tell the staff, "This is my daughter, the one I was telling you about with her master's degree in criminal justice." It broke my heart one day when I had to tell him I'd left the field in order to prioritize my family. Daddy seemed so disappointed in me and didn't seem to understand my reasoning. I knew that every ounce of his pride had been crushed when I broke that news to him and unfortunately, there wasn't much discussion about it after that. I just saw the sad look in my father's eyes and it was a look that I'll never forget.

All this time, I'd been updating momma about daddy's health issues, and in turn, she began applying more pressure on me, demanding that I tell him that I knew he wasn't my real father. My relationship with Jace had remained a thorn in momma's flesh. She'd never stopped reminding me that he wasn't my 'real' father, that I never belonged to his side of the family. She went so far as to tell me that he had no plans of including me in his Living Will. I would always tell her that I never expected anything from my father but his love and constantly relay to her that my greatest loss would be the loss of my father's physical existence. I would also relay to momma that there was no amount of money that could ever replace his presence in my life, so being included in his will was the least of my concerns.

I lived my entire life having to deal with the division that my mother created and trying my hardest to stand strong in displaying my genuine love and care for both of my parents, even though I often felt I was disrespecting momma's wishes. My love for my father was unconditional and there wasn't much my mother could do to change the way I felt about him. I refused to allow momma to permanently discourage me from maintaining a connection with my father.

Over a matter of months, daddy's health seemed to take a steep decline. Daddy was admitted into the hospital and had become very frail and ill, so with the health problems he was experiencing, the hospital staff kept daddy heavily sedated. During one visit I made to my father, he appeared to be in a very deep sleep. I began talking to him and telling him how much I had appreciated everything he had done for me and told him how much I loved him. As he rested peacefully in his hospital bed, I decided it was best to break the news to him while he was in a deep sleep, so I can at least tell my mother that I told him, even though I knew he wasn't conscious. That way, I didn't have to deal with the fact of hurting his feelings, so I did it... I followed momma's instruction by telling him I knew he wasn't my real father and that is when the unexpected occurred.

My father seemed to choke or gag and as a result, started coughing and I jumped back. I had hoped he was in such a deep sleep that he could not hear me, but his actions proved differently. Daddy heard everything and what I said had obviously disturbed him because he *was* indeed my father, regardless of how momma chose to see or accept it. I was so disappointed that I allowed myself to become caught up in such a horrible trap involving my mother's true feelings about my father. Daddy made a promise when he signed my birth certificate and remained true to his word by remaining by my side throughout my entire life, with the exception of the time that momma prevented me from seeing him.

Daddy was all I knew, so his "true" title didn't matter. Based on information often told to me by my mother, I was the one who felt my life was nothing but a lie that I had become caught up in. Although I felt satisfied and as though a huge burden had been lifted off of my back in sharing my knowledge of the matter involving my father's "true" relationship, I still felt deeply regretful. A form of regret that I'd carry for many years to follow.

I had finally granted my mother her wish and felt I had earned the ability to move forward with my life, as I continued to model unconditional love towards my father. The matter involving the "truth" was never brought up again, but I often felt cheated in life as a result of being pressured to clear up so many controversial matters that stemmed from decisions my mother made early on in her life. I absolutely hated being placed in the position of having to balance the love and respect I had for both of my parents.

As the days passed, I started preparing for my father's death mentally, emotionally and spiritually, especially in realizing the unlikeliness of my father ever returning home, although he believed he would return home someday. In order for daddy to have the ability to return home, he needed a ramp built up to the entrance of his home to make it wheelchair accessible. While in the hospital, daddy had developed gangrene in his leg, which in turn, had to be amputated. After having his leg removed, daddy never had the ability to stand up again and therefore, ended up bedridden. All of the hope I had for daddy's release and complete recovery had begun to diminish.

It was even more evident that daddy wasn't returning home when I went to visit him one day and he asked me to dial his phone number to confirm that the phone number he had for decades had been disconnected. Daddy was ex-tremely hurt and I know that is the time that he started to lose hope in his ability to return home. I didn't really have much of a relationship with my older siblings on my father's side and sure didn't feel comfortable questioning them about daddy's phone being disconnected, so I left it alone and continued to support daddy to the best of my ability from my end.

Daddy was holding on to every bit of life but it seemed that he was gradually being cut off and forced to accept the fact that his time was coming to an end. From our conversations, I knew daddy wasn't afraid to die, but at that point, even with his leg amputated, he wasn't ready to completely let go and I felt sad for him. He was always the type of person to give so much to others and in the end, I always believed he felt he was forgotten about.

Daddy's final days approached and as much as I attempted to prepare, I realized that I was not prepared for his death, or even prepared to deal with the family I was always told I didn't belong to. I only had a close relationship with my father and often felt alienated and disliked by relatives on my father's side. One of my greatest worries in relation to my father's passing was whether or not I would even be notified as soon as he passed, so I prayed for the opportunity to be with him until the end.

With the help provided by a nurse, daddy was able to make calls and during those times he had no success in reaching me, he would leave messages, requesting for me to pay him a visit. My family and I had just moved into a new home which was quite a ways outside of the city where daddy was receiving care. My father was in a nursing home and the trip from our new house would take me on a few highways. I wasn't familiar or comfortable with the route, so I relied heavily on my husband to take me back and forth.

In the days before my father died, my husband and I had listened to one of his messages. I had just opened my childcare business and Desmond and I were both working second jobs, but we knew we had to find some time to visit my dad. I happened to be assigned to a shift through my second job supervising a young teenage girl who had been admitted into the hospital. Ironically, the hospital happened to be located within the vicinity as the facility daddy was in. Desmond and I made plans for the whole family to visit my father as soon as my shift ended.

Desmond dropped me off for my shift, then went to run an errand with our kids. As soon as I checked in for my shift, I was informed the client I was scheduled to supervise had been discharged, so no further supervision was needed. I went back down to the hospital lobby and waited for Desmond. I sat there wondering how close I was to the care center where my father was staying. Having grown up in the city near the downtown area, I knew I was within close proximity, but just not sure how close.

When Desmond picked me up an hour later, we literally drove around the corner from the hospital to get to the nursing home where my father was staying. I could not believe how close the facility was to the hospital where I had been waiting for Desmond to return. I could have just walked over to the facility to see my dad. The good thing was that we, as a family had finally made it. I was so anxious and excited to finally see my father as we entered the elevator to go up to the floor he was staying on. I had finally made it down and I knew he would be so happy to see all of us.

After exiting the elevator, I approached the nurses' station and asked which room my father was in. One of the staff members paused and asked me to repeat my father's name. When I did, she paused then said, "Your father just expired a few minutes ago. I am so sorry."

I couldn't seem to make out what she was saying. I had never heard the term "expired" used to describe death and those certainly weren't the words I had expected to hear. I had missed the final opportunity to see my father alive and he had missed seeing me. I had let him down, once again. I was numb.

The staff asked me if I desired to see my father's deceased body and I sorrowfully accepted. Desmond decided to take our kids back to the car and the nurse led me into the room where my father's body was lying. I stood next to his bed and stared at his lifeless body. As I stood there, a Chaplin entered the room and asked me if I was okay. I said I was, then he offered to pray with me. As he started praying, I gently placed my hand on my father's body. During the prayer, my father's body jerked. I am not sure of the exact cause, but scientifically, it means that the muscles in the body are relaxing. In the spiritual sense for me, it meant my father was aware that I had come to see him. I was at peace. I remained there until my oldest sister, Charmaine on my father's side arrived. Charmaine always seemed to have a positive attitude about life and together, we stood at daddy's bedside sharing a few words. I was completely saddened. I knew this day was coming, but I wasn't sure how I would make it through.

The next few days following daddy's death was somewhat of a blur for me. It was a time in my life that I dreaded facing the most, primarily in knowing that I was most connected to my father and knew that once I lost him, I would most-likely lose my connection with everyone on his side of the family. I also had no idea how I was going to get through his funeral and send my final farewell. I spent many days leading up to my father's funeral reading my Bible and reciting the 23rd Psalm to get me through.

My father's passing occurred just days before momma's birthday and coincidentally, he was buried a day after her birthday. When my husband and I arrived to my father's funeral with our children, I made up my mind that I was going to share my true feelings about how great of an "adoptive" father Jace had been to me and when the time came, I took the opportunity to speak to all who had attended. I stood up and expressed how much I appreciated everything my father had done for me and also expressed how much I admired his "real" manhood in stepping up to be such a great father to me by adopting me.

For so long I had been pushed by my mother to bring the story she had always shared with me to light. A story I always believed others in the family suspected or knew, but soon learned at the funeral that no one had any knowledge of me being adopted by my father because daddy had never discussed it with anyone. After daddy's funeral, not only had I lost the only father I knew, but also the relationship I shared with the family I had known all of my life.

After sharing my revelation at his funeral. I felt horrible and as though I had caused irreparable damage. Everyone in attendance seemed shocked. One member of the family went so far as to call me after daddy's funeral to curse me out for being so disrespectful and seeming as though I desired to completely cut my family out of my life. I really didn't know which way to turn and believed it was only best for me to turn away completely because I had ruined my father's image. My decision to speak at my father's funeral and say all that I said was something I would have to learn to live with the remainder of my life.

Before deciding to completely close that door to the only real family I had ever known during my young years, I created frames containing the scripture of the 23rd Psalm to deliver to members of my family on daddy's side and this was a difficult task to take on when I arrived to deliver a frame to Charmaine who had moved into the home that I always knew as daddy's home.

When I entered the home, everyone seemed very happy to see me and Charmaine introduced me to one of her friends who happened to be sitting in the same chair that daddy always sat in to take his insulin shots. It pierced my heart to see this man sitting in my father's chair and turned out to be one of the most difficult times that I had faced following daddy's death. When I walked out of my father's house that last time, I knew I would not be returning. I could not stand to bear the pain in knowing that I would never be able to see or visit him again.

My relationship with my mother went through a small transformation after my father passed.

Momma happened to be walking home one day when she crossed paths with a gentleman by the name of Mr. Johnson. He invited her to come and visit during one of his Sunday services at the church where he served as Bishop. Momma gladly accepted and by that next Sunday, she was in attendance at the church she would soon become a member of.

Bishop Johnson displayed so much genuine love towards my mother that she had seldom received from others. For example, momma started having major issues with the house she was renting. First, there was a break-in and robbery that left her feeling very anxious about her safety. Shortly after the robbery, she noticed large sections of paint beginning to bubble up and peel off from the walls. Momma had the area checked and was told there was a massive amount of mold growing on the walls. She found out the property owners had knowledge of the situation before she'd moved in but instead of fixing it, they'd simply painted over it.

After hearing what momma was going through, Bishop Johnson offered momma one of the church-owned, rental properties located across the street from the church for her to move into. As a testament to my mother's faith in Bishop Johnson, she accepted the offer without hesitation. Momma did not trust people easily, so once Bishop Johnson gained her trust, he had won a soul and a friend for life

I had always understood their arrangement to be that momma could remain in the property for as long as Bishop Johnson was alive. He must have made special arrangements for her because when he passed some years later, momma was blessed to remain as a tenant until she herself, passed away.

It was their friendship and momma's dedication to that church that fueled my own spiritual growth and provided a space for the two of us to reconnect after my father's death. The commitment she'd made to improving her life, while a member of the church exposed me to the light of salvation.

When she passed, I was left with an overwhelming abundance of faith and trust in the Lord. I had witnessed my mother survive through so much hell that severely impacted her health and wellbeing, but she came through in the end as a result of learning there was no better way for her to remove the darkness out of our lives than by surrendering and committing her life to the Lord. Momma accepted the Lord as her Savior and truly believed in the teachings of the Bible. She came to believe that all of her sins had been washed away. Although it posed as a struggle at times, momma learned to search for the light, in the midst of the darkness.

By the strength modeled through momma, I learned to put forth my best effort in doing everything possible to break through what seemed to be many unbearable challenges of life. With the disappointment that both of my parents had in me as a teenager preparing to bring a baby into the world, they matured in understanding that the responsibility I had in having to care for my child was for my good and would serve a great deal in contributing so much to bringing me out of so much darkness. I am so thankful that daddy never completely turned his back on me. I believe he knew how much his unconditional love meant to me because I proved how much I loved and cared for him by passing his name on to CJ. In daddy's way of expressing his excitement, he ordered a bunch of pencils with the inscription of CJ's full name on them.

What I never allowed to break me in life, made me a much stronger person and momma acknowledged my strength just prior to her passing when she requested to meet with me and CJ. Momma admitted that she was ashamed of what others would think of her as a parent after I broke the news to her about my pregnancy at such an early age, which she relayed as her reasoning for so much of the harsh treatment displayed towards me.

Momma also relayed that my pregnancy was a struggle for her to accept because she had her own dreams and aspirations for my life, later recognizing the fact that it was *my* life that *I* needed to live. Momma also explained to us that after choosing to give her life to the Lord, she realized that my early pregnancy was what I needed to happen in order for me to get my life on track. From that moment forward, momma struggled with a lot of guilt, frequently apologizing to me and asking for forgiveness for anything she had ever done to hurt me. I constantly reassured momma that I had forgiven her long ago.

As momma was preparing for death, my greatest hope and prayer was to be blessed with the opportunity to stand by her side as she transitioned into afterlife. Since I'd missed that opportunity with my father, it was very important to me to be there with my mother.

My prayer was granted. As I stood next to momma's bedside, I got to sing some of her favorite church songs to her and told her how much I loved her. Momma didn't get to see Jeris before she passed, which she desired so badly, so I promised momma that Jeris would be taken care of and that we would all meet up again when our time came to pass on.

My words seemed to keep momma comforted as she prepared to take her final breath just moments before her 64th birthday. I watched the clock carefully, asking momma to hang on until her birthday so I could sing *"Happy Birthday"* to her. She seemed to struggle with breathing, but held on. At 12:01 a.m., Desmond happened to call from work to see how momma was doing. Knowing that momma was preparing to take her final breath, I immediately and gently placed the phone up against momma's ear. Desmond was the last to be heard by momma before taking her final breath of life. Momma had passed on and Desmond was extremely sad as we disconnected. The date that was always celebrated as momma's birthday had now become the date that would be known as the date she had been called back home and I was blessed to sing *"Happy Birthday"* to my mother, one final time.

I found, having to learn to live in this huge world without the existence of both of my parents was extremely difficult.

Even though I had my immediate family, I still had such a void in my life. A very huge part of my past had been permanently put to rest and in dealing with the pain and sorrow of searching for closure in my life, I had to remember how important it was to remain strong in my emotional and mental state of mind, primarily for the sole purpose of my children and also in my effort to continue growing stronger. Without the existence of my parents, I knew it would be a crucial step for me in **Learning to Release the Beast** that manifested within.

19

Learning to Release the Beast

The conversation was intense over a controversial matter my husband and I were discussing in relation to the differences involving our parenting styles on the eve of May 29th, 2011. I recall the date so vividly because it was one of the few dates I struggled with as I approached the death anniversaries for both of my parents.

In our distinctive parenting roles it was typical for Desmond to take on more of the stern parenting role, with me being more of the easygoing and understanding parent when it came to rationalizing about our children, in order to gain a better understanding of their point of view. But it wasn't always like that and in fact, very early on, when CJ was a teenager in high school, Desmond noticed a change in CJ's behavior. CJ had always been a quiet and very well mannered child, but he had grown to become extremely silent, to the point that he was not expressing his feelings at all. While I thought nothing of it, assuming it was just typical teenage behavior coupled with CJ's personality type, Desmond picked up on it quick and brought it to my attention. I had unconsciously learned to adapt more to that "tough love" spirit that momma used with me when I was CJ's age, so for months and possibly even years, I was unaware that CJ had a streak of anger manifesting inside.

It wasn't until CJ and I had a discussion that I learned that he was holding onto a grudge regarding some past decisions I'd made in allowing certain men into our lives, in my effort to "rescue" them; Davis, in particular. CJ never felt comfortable about me inviting Davis into my life. At one point shortly after I'd started seeing Davis, CJ took a look at Davis and whispered, "That's Davis? He looks like the devil". Needless to say the initial introduction didn't go well with CJ and Davis. I walked away from the brief relationship I had with Davis, not realizing that the effects of my decision to have him in my life would cause years of pain for my son.

So, there CJ and I were, standing in the kitchen having a discussion, when the words came out of his mouth. "I am angry at you for dating that guy. I knew he wasn't good for you, but you never listened when I tried to tell you!"

CJ's words were like a rake cutting through my soul. What had I done and why had I allowed Davis into my life? What purpose did it ever serve? I had allowed my son to develop many of the same feelings towards Davis as I had towards Hades, also knowing Hades was a bad man for momma, but momma just couldn't see it.

It dawned on me too, that CJ was around seven when Davis and I were together, which was the same age I was when I began to see so much of the darkness in Hades. Momma had chosen to ignore what I saw in Hades, and I had ignored the darkness that CJ saw in Davis.

I exploded in frustration and CJ replied with, "See... that's why I can't talk to you!"

It was a moment I never forgot and also the moment that changed our lives as a family for years to follow. I made the decision to learn to talk to my children and make more of an effort to listen to their pain whenever they chose to express their feelings, but on that evening of May 29th, everything had changed.

That day marked the ten year anniversary of my father's death and I realized that the death anniversaries of both of my parents hitting so close together served as a trigger for me. I also struggled with the reality of momma taking her final breath on her birthday, which I had initially begged for her to do, not realizing it would cause years of mixed emotions as I continued to mourn her death.

So, here I was, approaching momma and daddy's death anniversaries, in a mourning state of mind. I was still learning to deal with the harsh reality of the pain of accepting the fact that momma was gone forever and would never again return in the flesh. I no longer had momma around to speak on a deep and spiritual level with and had lost those days of momma speaking such encouraging words over me. Nor would I ever be able to smell the sweet scent I had always smelled during moments I hugged my mother.

The most difficult of all was, I would never have the opportunity to talk to her and ask her "Why?" regarding so many issues that arose in my life that we never had a chance to deal with because momma did not like to openly express her true feelings and frankly, could not stand to discuss anything about her past life. But, I had reached a stage in my life where I desired answers and the one source with all of the answers was no longer living. I was angry and I started carrying a lot of baggage, which often contributed to bouts of crying, or an eruption of my anger.

My anger had grown out of control and momma was no longer around to comfort and keep me grounded by consoling me, expressing an understanding about what I was experiencing, or guiding me to know how to best deal with my problems. I no longer had that source of support that I had managed to lean on for so many years; the source primarily responsible for the core of my anger. My anger seemed to take control of my world and I felt completely helpless.

With our differentiated views, Desmond and I realized there was no room for budging from either of us, so unfortunately, a consensus was never reached relating to our parenting stance that evening. Sure, it may not have been that serious and also could have been dealt with the next day, but my anger had reached its peak and I wanted to deal with our conflict at that very moment.

Desmond was fairly relaxed at the time as he explained his view during our debate. We were having a discussion about how we were raising our children and what our expectations were. Of course, I was more worked up, not so much due to the fact of not agreeing, but more related to the fact that I was struggling to get through a stage of mourning. The matter seemed to intensify and I reached my boiling point and my anger erupted, just like that of a volcano.

Desmond had stepped into the position as my sole supporter in helping me deal with my anger, but this time we were struggling to see eye to eye. I so badly needed the woman who taught me to be angry and ignited that fire inside of me and since I didn't have her to fill that void, times had become difficult for me.

While attempting to develop strength in learning how to effectively deal with the death anniversaries of my parents, I was also trying to establish a path of my own to follow since momma wasn't around to guide me through. I had to find a way to make it mentally, emotionally and spiritually.

Those specific "roles" that led up to our debate derived from Desmond once suggesting that we take on the good cop and bad cop parenting styles in our effort to establish more of a balance with our children, which is how I ended up in the role as the understanding parent and Desmond as the stern parent, but since our roles unexpectedly switched, it triggered a major conflict.

Over the years, I had grown to become weary in dealing with the challenges of life and completely annoyed with the responsibilities of parenting. I just desired for everything to always go right, so I didn't have to face the misery, disappointment and discouragement in trying to be that perfect parent. It was a time I needed my husband to understand my point of view as the "bad cop" and desired for him to join my side in order for me to feel that married union of support we had spent so much time in our lives sharing. Unfortunately the issue mounted from a molehill into a mountain.

This turned out to be an evening that I learned a lot about myself and realized that I had to figure out how to break away from the shackles that seemed to have my soul so tightly bounded. With momma no longer around to help loosen the chains of bondage and provide me with a little relief, I had accepted that I was completely on my own and had to travel through what felt like a maze to find my way out.

During our debate, I noticed that my son Carter, my daughter Janiece and my younger son, Devante were all staring at me with blank looks on their faces, as if they were wondering what had gotten into me. The house was completely silent and I realized I needed to take a break from my family. I felt as though I had let them down by allowing my anger to get the best of me, by arguing extensively over a matter with my husband that wasn't a huge deal to begin with. I knew I had reached a breaking point in my life with so much of the pain that had been surfacing and also as a result of so many unanswered questions that I was forced to find answers to on my own. It also didn't help that I had no connection, involvement, or support available to me from extended family members who

I felt could understand my pain well enough to guide me through the struggles I was facing.

I decided it was best to leave and take a time out, to avoid affecting my husband and children any more than I already had. Little did I know, by that time the damage had already been done. I was in tears and had to get out as fast as I could and as far away as I could. I felt as though my kids no longer knew their mom and I sure didn't like the person I had become. I wondered how it would even be possible for me to continue carrying on with so much embedded anger.

I took the keys to our vehicle and stormed out of the house, not wanting to be followed, or even located. I had no idea where I was going and really didn't want to return. I had reached one of my lowest moments and there was no one who had the ability to get me out of the dark headspace I was in.

When I left the house, the first stop I made was to the cemetery to visit my father's grave. I desired so badly to reconnect with my father in any possible way, but all I had was a huge, wide headstone to sit near, with daddy's name and the names of other relatives engraved on it. The scripture of John 3:16, "For God so loved the world that he gave his only begotten Son, that whosoever believeth in him should not perish, but have everlasting life", was also engraved on daddy's headstone, a scripture from the Bible that he had selected.

During outings with my father, he would always drive down the busy street that the cemetery set off of and point out his headstone to show me where he would be buried someday. I had no idea that I would be driving to the cemetery as an older adult to visit my deceased father's grave site. Daddy always had to have the best of everything, which meant the largest and best-looking headstone that was visible to everyone, even strangers. So, by daddy's constant reminders I knew exactly where to go and I believe that was his sole purpose, knowing that he would have to leave me behind someday.

As I entered the cemetery and slowly drove up to his burial site, holding onto the many memories that my father left me with, my tears began to stream down heavily. I missed my daddy dearly and wished so badly that I had him around to talk to, but he was gone forever and I had to figure out a way to cope.

After sitting there for a while, I began to hear strange noises and felt as if I wasn't alone. It was late spring and the flowers were starting to bloom, so I assumed the noises were caused by a squirrel that was nearby. The noise disrupted the quiet time I was attempting to create for myself and instead, created a sense of uneasiness, so I decided to leave the cemetery and continue driving, with no desire to return home.

My eyes were still filled with tears as I drove in the direction of the home I grew up in as a young child and teenager. When I located the home we had once resided in, I parked my car right in front of the house and reminisced on my darkest days. I reflected on the past troubles and struggles I had experienced from the age of nine through sixteen. It wasn't long before I realized how far along I had come since those troublesome years of my life. By then, it was pitch dark and I started to develop an eerie feeling while sitting in my parked vehicle, so I decided to take off and find another place to visit, still having no desire to return home.

As I drove away, I began to count my blessings. I also valued the fact in knowing at one point, I had no way to escape from the horror that I experienced in that neighborhood when I was a child, but as an adult, I did. I had the freedom and ability to drive away at my own leisure and was no longer trapped in a lifestyle that once posed as a struggle for me to get through.

Although it took some time for me to notice, I came to the realization that my life had improved and all of the dreams that I had for myself had actually come true. I had also realized that I was able to escape the trauma I had experienced while living in that house and neighborhood. A neighborhood that at that time, was filled with extreme violence and where substance abusers could be found, hanging out on just about every corner.

Inside our home wasn't much different. There was violence and substance abuse. My very own great uncle, known as Uncle Charles was an alcoholic. We would often hear him tumbling down the steps of his basement apartment every single night in a drunken stupor. One of those nights turned out to be the final time we'd hear Uncle Charles fall. After a couple of nights of not hearing Uncle Charles, momma got the keys to check on him and found Uncle Charles curled up at the bottom of the steps, dead.

In my deep thoughts as I drove around town, having no idea where my next destination would be, I began to wonder what the purpose was in driving to areas where I had spent so many dark days. I couldn't help but wonder if it was even worth it because so much of my pain had begun to resurface. Even though I was able to reflect on my past life and count my blessings with the ability to drive away, I started to feel as though my past was beginning to haunt me, so I picked up on my speed as I continued to drive away.

I was finally coming around and could see how much of the light I had actually traveled through. I was living a much healthier lifestyle than what I had been exposed to. I just had the difficult task of exploring creative ways to continue making effective and positive changes that would serve as a benefit for me and my family.

My final destination that night was passing by the last home my mother lived in, prior to her death. As I drove through the neighborhood she lived in, I visualized myself standing at the front door, knocking and waiting for my mother to come to the door. I could see myself entering and exiting through the front door of her home during the numerous visits I paid to momma.

I also spent time reminiscing about the day my mother requested to meet with me and my then, fiancé, after expressing his desire to marry me. When we arrived, momma pulled out some chairs and the three of us sat on the porch together as momma spoke to us and explained the reason for requesting the meeting.

Momma told us she had prayed about what she wanted to talk to us about and knew she was doing the right thing in following through. Momma's first words were, "Desmond, before you marry my daughter, there is something you should know…"

I looked at my mother and initially felt she was attempting to sabotage my engagement and future wedding, but I allowed her to continue.

Momma proceeded to tell Desmond that I had an anger problem that I needed to work on and that she needed him to know before we took the steps in walking down the aisle to exchange our vows. Desmond was very polite towards momma, as he respectfully listened and expressed his understanding of the matter and also of her concern. She didn't seem convinced initially, but accepted his response and our meeting ended. We stayed to visit for a while longer before leaving. What Desmond failed to relay to my mother was the fact that I reminded him a lot of his own mother, so momma's warning was nothing surprising for him because he was confident that he knew what he was getting into.

As previously mentioned, Desmond had witnessed my anger for the first time, during my final year of graduate school. We were excitedly planning our wedding for the following spring, which would've provided me the time needed to complete Graduate school, as I was scheduled to graduate that following May. Instead, our wedding plans were bumped up to a winter month during my Christmas break after learning I was expecting our child. My stress had reached its peak after becoming worried that I would not be able to attain my goal in graduating from school on time. Another issue was the fact that I had decided against having any additional children since CJ was close to turning nine years old at the time. With everything I had going on, I just didn't feel that I was mentally and emotionally prepared to bring a new baby into our lives so early in our marriage.

While I do believe Desmond was a bit surprised by how angry I had become slightly caught off-guard, it certainly wasn't serious enough to disrupt our engagement and wedding plans. We have since celebrated nearly 22 years of marriage and having been blessed with a large family has provided me with true meaning and purpose.

After pulling away from the property where momma last resided, I made up my mind that I would find a way deal with my anger on my own, by finding clever ways to create and establish more peace in my life, as I continued to embrace motherhood. I still seemed to be bounded by chains and knew it would take a lot of effort for me to break through what momma often referred to as a 'generational curse'. It was solely up to me to work towards repairing the harm caused by others I had developed trust in.

After a long night of driving, I made it back home to my family where I felt safe. A place of comfort that brought me happiness during the times I refused to allow the dark spirit of anger to control my emotions. I realized how blessed I was and decided that I was going to continue pressing forward and counting my blessings, no matter what. I had made up my mind that I was going to continue striving to create a difference that involved positive changes for the betterment of myself and the beautiful and loving family I had been blessed with.

I set out to find my true identity, after years of being told by momma, "You don't belong", while continuing to seek happiness.

My ability to fully complete this book was a very reward-ing and therapeutic experience for me because it blessed me with the ability to retrace my steps and validate the positive ending to my struggles. I've been able to reflect on my past circumstances and recognize how many of those experiences served to impact my life in such positive ways. I would occasionally hear from others that it is not a good practice to focus on the past, but rather look ahead, to prevent feelings of discouragement, but for me, having the ability to look back and reflect on my past challenges has created a sense of strength in my ability to continue moving forward in a productive manner. For me, looking back at my past life was like looking through a rearview mirror from the inside of an automobile while driving away. Although my experience was very hurtful, it was also enlightening to know that I survived and made it through.

There were a lot of people that I had crossed paths with in my lifetime who made every attempt to break me down, which has been near to impossible, due to the battles I've learned to fight in my life along the way, so there really isn't much that can be done to me to discourage me and cause me to feel I am not worthy enough. I've learned that my life is just as important as anyone else's life and because of that reason, will always have my mind, heart and soul set on **Fulfilling a Purposeful Journey.**

20

Fulfilling a Purposeful Journey

Dedicating my future to serving the juvenile population was how I desired to spend the remainder of my life. I saw it as a way of giving back to the community, while seeking my own personal self-gratification in my effort to save children, by assisting them to get through the dark times of their adolescent years. So, that is what I set out to do after enrolling in college.

Some of my fondest memories include the involvement of two very influential teachers from the last and most challenging elementary school that I attended.

The first was my fifth grade teacher from Chicago, IL named Ms. Gettys who had a reputation of being very intimidating, strict and well respected. The students assigned to Ms. Gettys class were all destined to learn because she maintained a very structured environment.

As we approached the end of that school year, Ms. Gettys pulled me aside and asked me if I'd like to meet two of her nieces from Chicago who were planning to visit over the summer. I never knew why she only selected me for a playdate with her nieces, but I was ecstatic to accept her offer and when the time came for Ms. Getty's to pick me up, I had one of the most memorable times. What was most rewarding was having the ability to spend time with my teacher and see her as a regular person and not the strict teacher she was best known for.

Over the years, I ended up crossing paths with Ms. Gettys again after my mother found out that Ms. Gettys was her next door neighbor. Ms. Getty's and I arranged a visit so she could meet my son, CJ. That following summer I reunited with Ms. Gettys nieces who had arrived in town for their annual summer visit to Colorado and we spent some time together, taking pictures and reminiscing about the time we first met during our elementary years. As a young mom, life had dramatically changed for me and since I lived on my own, I rarely saw Ms. Gettys, who still managed to maintain a close relationship with momma up until momma passed away.

The other teacher who impacted my life was my physical education teacher named Ms. Oaks, who had a tough spirit and a gift for identifying strengths and pushing kids to reach their full potentials with the God-given talents that she identified.

Ms. Oaks identified my strength in speed racing and placed me on a relay team with all boys… many of the same boys who had teased and bullied me when I first enrolled as a new student. The male dominated team I was placed on broke many school records with the relays we ran and we were constantly awarded for our talent, even earning the Presidential Award for our speed that was signed by former President Ronald Reagan.

By the end of that school year, Ms. Oaks invited me to join her track team. I didn't know much about track and field, but accepted her offer and Ms. Oaks would swing by to pick me up for track meets on weekends and even encouraged my mother to attend one of the meets. I was so excited for momma to attend because momma had very little awareness of my physical talents since I wasn't involved in any other sports or outside activities. That particular day I had set my standards high because I desired to make momma proud of me.

There momma was, sitting in the bleachers of the stadium as I was preparing to run my race to the finish line. It was a national track meet, so I was running against others in my bracket from across the United States.

The time came for me to step up to the mark and as I was preparing to run, I looked up and saw momma and Ms. Oaks sitting there with their eyes locked on me. I had planned to run my hardest.

The gunshot sounded and I took off. I was in the lead and all of a sudden, I felt the presence of another runner catching up with me. She breezed right by me and I was so hurt and angry. My way of responding was refusing to cross the finish line and instead, came to an abrupt stop with my arms crossed, crying and pouting in frustration.

As I stood there with tears in my eyes, I heard Ms. Oaks and many others yelling for me to keep going and cross the finish line, but I ignored all of them. My race had been defeated by a girl from Texas who stole my first place title. I didn't realize at the time that I passed up a spot for second place, which still would've made momma proud of me.

She'd taken off from her weekend job to attend my track meet to watch me run and was satisfied with that alone, but I was too young to appreciate that fact. Unfortunately, that was the last track meet I attended and the last track team I had ever joined, but not the last time I hung out with Ms. Oaks.

Ms. Oaks and I remained in close contact throughout the years that followed and she took on more of a mentoring role in my life. After becoming pregnant, I confided in Ms. Oaks and asked for her advice on what I should do. Ms. Oaks sounded a bit reluctant to share her point of view, but developed the courage to advise me to get an abortion so I could pursue a college career.

After making the decision to keep my baby and moving away from momma, I never spoke to Ms. Oaks again or arranged a time for her to see my baby. I was deeply offended that she had joined sides with everyone else who believed they knew what was best for me at the time.

Well, Ms. Oaks seemed to not believe that I could attend college with a baby, but I did and I graduated with a degree that allowed me to go out and be of good service to others.

As a young mom, I set out on my personal mission to give back to the adolescent population. One of the most rewarding jobs I had was serving as a counselor and client manager for the youth and young adult population.

Unfortunately, I had to quit the job I loved the most, as a client manager, due to life changing circumstances. After delivering three additional children, Carter, Janiece and Devante into the world, my husband and I experienced an unexpected pregnancy with our youngest child, Malachi. The challenge in adjusting to a new child was difficult for us. Travel to and from work for nearly an hour or more each way had become a bit too much. Gas was high and the cost of infant care was outrageous. After calculating our expenses, it became evident that we were spending more money for me to continue working, so in an effort to balance out our finances, I sadly resigned to begin a new life, which turned out to be a blessing because it provided me with more quality time as a mom to my newborn and other children.

Up until that point, every single job I'd had that granted me the opportunity to work with kids was rewarding in its own unique way because it provided me with a chance to give back.

There were three kids who positively impacted my job the most in such rewarding ways and blessed me with that drive to keep performing at my best. I worked for the district attorney's office and one of them was a client named Jacob who resided in a high-risk area. Jacob was fifteen years old and truly valued his education. He took pride in attending school, but his mother could not afford to purchase a backpack for Jacob to carry his books back and forth, so I put in a request for a backpack through my job that I could donate to him.

Jacob was so thankful for his backpack that he returned to one of our scheduled sessions with a fancy drinking glass that he'd purchased from the Dollar Store. He told me he was able to purchase the glass after scraping some change together. It was the only way he felt he could show his appreciation for the backpack that I ordered for him. That fancy drinking glass became a cherished keepsake of mine for years to follow. I will never forget how much Jacob's beautiful blue eyes lit up when I handed him his backpack filled with school supplies. For Jacob, it was definitely the small things that mattered.

I had another high-risk client named Juan who attended that same school. Juan was an active gang member who continuously encountered problems at school to the point that the school was placed on lockdown and the doors chained shut, with a helicopter hovering over the school one day, as a result of another student reporting that Juan allegedly stated he was going to shoot up the school.

It was expected of every client in our program to report any contact they encountered with the law during their participation in the program, so when Juan arrived to my office, he made certain to report that he was questioned by law enforcement over the alleged accusation, but later released when no evidence was found. Juan and I spent the remainder of our time during our session that day discussing alternative ways of handling similar situations with conflictual matters as such.

A few weeks later, Juan relayed to me that he had gotten jumped and stabbed in his leg by the same group of rival gang members who he believed used a knife or spiked brass knuckles to cause the injuries. Juan showed me his wounds and we spent time discussing a safety plan in the case that he should encounter any further problems.

Life eventually got better for Juan after he found a girlfriend and settled down. During one of our sessions, Juan brought an airbrushed painting, containing the design of a large heart with the most beautiful pastel colors. During previous sessions, Juan would frequently share stories with me about his talent in airbrush painting and express his plan on showing his artwork firsthand, and that is just what he did. After sharing the image of his airbrushed painting with me, he told me that the painting was for me to keep. This was another treasure that I cherished. It is framed and currently hanging up on my bedroom wall to remind me of the kind spirit he continued to display during his struggle to survive.

The third client named Douglas was also 15 years old and considered to be 'odd', per information provided by a school administrator who strongly believed Douglas was capable of shooting up the school. I never allowed the school administrator's opinion to influence how I felt about Douglas. Instead, I perceived Douglas to be a very kind hearted person who was unique in his own way, as many of us are. The school administrator had nothing to use against Douglas but her suspicion, so I respectfully documented her concerns and continued to work towards successfully progressing with Douglas.

Douglas' mother was well aware of how he was being treated and perceived by the school administration and desired nothing less than for Douglas to succeed. She felt their judgmental attitudes were going to discourage him. This information relayed to me by Douglas' mother provided me with a sense of direction in effectively working with Douglas in an effort to build up his confidence and in the end, it worked out, but took some time to get there.

Douglas wasn't initially easy to work with, due to the barriers he had built up for authority figures in his life. During many of our initial sessions, Douglas displayed somewhat of a distant behavior towards me and one day, caught me off-guard shortly after the start of one of our scheduled sessions. Douglas politely asked me to tell him what we discussed during his last session, without reviewing my notes, which had occurred two weeks prior. This was quite easy for me to do because it was always imperative for me to strive towards developing personal relationships with every single client on my caseload. After making his request, I asked Douglas for his reasoning behind such a request and he replied with, "People don't listen to me and I don't think you even listen to me, so if you can tell me what we discussed during the last session, I'll know that you listen to me."

I looked at him and smiled and began to tell him what we discussed during the last session. He appeared taken aback and responded with, "You really do listen to me."

While it should be a common practice to review notes prior to sessions, I seldom had that opportunity because my appointments were often booked back-to-back and it made it even worse if one of my clients arrived late. If I didn't have the personal relationship that I did with my assigned clientele, I would have made more of an effort to follow through with that common practice, but it wasn't necessary for me. I knew the life of every client on my caseload, so my ability to recall a conversation was never a problem for me.

After Douglas realized how important he, as an individual was to me, his guards completely came down and he started opening up and sharing more with me.

Douglas told me that he liked to draw and had a picture of a woman's face that he had planned to share with me. I told him I was excited and looking forward to checking out his drawing during our next session.

When Douglas returned two weeks later, he informed me that he didn't bring the picture of the woman's face and instead, decided to bring a different picture to the session that he'd drawn specifically for me. He said he didn't know the meaning of it, or why he drew it, but relayed that he wanted me to have it. Douglas pulled out a folder from his backpack and handed me the most beautiful picture of a forearm and hand. The forearm had a vine wrapped around it, extending down to the hand that was holding a branch attached to a small bushel of grapes.

I was stunned by this image in the picture and told him that it meant a lot to me. I also told him about my mother passing and shared with him that I had been reading the Bible from start to finish for comfort ever since. I told Douglas that the image had a very deep and spiritual meaning and expressed my plans on searching for the meaning from my Bible that evening after I returned home. It was at that time that Douglas stood up and reached in his pocket and pulled out a little pocket Bible and shared with me that he also made it a point to read his Bible.

When I went home that night, I opened my Bible and came across the verse in John 15:5 which states, "I am the vine, ye are the branches: He that abideth in me, and I in him, the same bringeth forth much fruit: for without me ye can do nothing."

I knew that this image and scripture was for me and that I was serving my true purpose in serving the lives of our youth. I made copies of Douglas' drawing and pinned his original drawing up on the wall right next to my bed, where it still remains today.

There was a time in my life that I believed I had closed my doors for good in serving the adolescent population, but as a result of a situation that arose, involving my teenage son, Devante, during his middle school years, I made the decision to start my own outreach business to provide services geared towards strengthening our young people who continue to experience the everyday struggles of life, while attempting to establish their own ground and sense of identity. I know and will always believe that my calling is built around serving our adolescent population in the most effective manner. After all, it's what I know best.

What's sad about the situation involving our young people is that there are so many young souls hurting and the issues are clearly being overlooked. We are living in a new era and time and the pressures that so many of our young people are dealing with are severe and unfortunately, the funding for services is not as accessible as it once was many years ago. Once we, as a society truly learn about **The Value of Life**, life in general will become that much more rewarding and meaningful.

21

The Value of Life

As a maturing adult I learned to value life more for what it was worth, which wasn't so easy for me to do in consideration of the lingering pain I had buried so deep within, stemming from my childhood years. At times, I felt a sense of emptiness and often perceived portions of my life as that of a dark cloud periodically hovering over me. There were times I would fall into a depression, or become enraged and I knew if I didn't learn to view the value of my life as "half full" from the image of the glass filled with liquid, that there was a great chance of losing my battle filled with faith, hope and strength.

I had to learn to find a way to deal with my past in the healthiest of manners. I found that the best way for me to make this possible involved developing the strength I needed and desired through my own spiritual growth. My spirituality that I had learned to adapt to was not anything that was taught to me. More or less, it was the embedded knowledge and understanding of good versus evil, quite similar to many of the stories that are recorded in the Bible and I knew I was destined to follow my heart by selecting the good over evil and through that experience, I have learned to value and love life at its best.

I frequently heard in my lifetime, "No one ever said life would be easy" and since we only get one life, I figured I would try and make the best out of it by learning to live my life to the fullest. Without the experience of overcoming challenges and obstacles, how would it be possible for me to encourage others?

For the longest, I had learned to bury my pain, trying to survive the best way I knew how, but the experience did nothing for the true self that I was hiding. My experience was like living my life in falsehood and I knew I was not being true to myself by holding onto so much that could serve to be a testimony to others, young or aged, who may be experiencing much of the same pain.

For so long, I forced myself to live with the scabbed wounds that seemed to open up from time to time and I realized, in order to continue growing and prospering, I had to do what was necessary to release my pain and that is by taking the steps necessary to let my pain go. In selecting to hold on to my pain, I knew I was only permitting my life to remain under the full control of what I consider as chains of bondage and I refuse to allow this pain to remain dormant in my heart, spirit and soul.

After developing the ability to maneuver around obstacles placed in my path, I've learned that life in general can be such a beautiful experience. Learning to survive many of the challenges in life is truly about how we choose to deal with the obstacles we encounter. Life is far too precious to allow the challenges to overrule our destinies.

Because I value the lives of others, I have decided to go public with my story in hopes that it reaches some of the most discouraged souls who struggle with the belief that there is no way out when the days seem the darkest. I've learned to chase the happiness that I saw in others and always desired to have.

Over the years, I have learned to take pride in and appreciate life for everything it has to offer. Life certainly wasn't an easy slate for me during my childhood years and after spending so much time viewing the deceased bodies of childhood friends and others I didn't know, it provided me with a strong drive to keep fighting for survival.

I will never forget the time I read the story about the death of two sisters who had been murdered by their mom's boyfriend. I, myself was 12 at the time and desired to see the bodies of both girls' because I felt a deep sense of connection, so I walked down to the mortuary alone, located just a few blocks away from our home. These young souls had lost their lives making an attempt to protect their mother, which I was able to relate very well to. The girls were 12 and 14 years old and they were both stabbed to death by their mother's boyfriend during a domestic violence dispute. The mother survived and had to live with the fact in knowing that the lives of her baby girls were lost in their attempt to protect her; the one soul that was placed on this earth to protect them.

I was so saddened to read about these sisters losing their lives because it hit so close to home for me. Viewing their lifeless bodies caused me to reminisce on how my life had been as a child living with Hades. Momma and I had been blessed to have survived being abused, these poor girls had not. The attacks that had been inflicted upon the girls were so brutal that the mortician used clear plastic during their open casket viewing, in an effort to conceal many of the stab wounds inflicted upon the upper parts of their bodies.

Then there was the senseless death of Mrs. Richards' daughter. Mrs. Richards was one of the lunch ladies at my elementary school. She would always serve me a little extra of my favorite foods. One day, Mrs. Richards saw me walking home from school with a friend and pulled up next to the curb where we were walking and asked if she could take us to the shoe store to purchase new shoes. It was just the type of person Mrs. Richards was, so we gladly accepted. On the way to the shoe store, she stopped to pick her daughter, Andrea up from school. Coincidentally, it was the same Catholic school I attended during my second and third grade year, prior to momma pulling me out to attend public school. Andrea was a very cute and sweet little girl who appeared shy and said very little to us other than "Hi", as she bashfully looked away. Mrs. Richards then drove us to a shoe store and bought us a new pair of shoes. It was one of the kindest gestures that a random adult had done for me and I always cherished that day.

A few years later, I heard about the death of a little girl who was riding her bike with some friends. It turned out that it was Mrs. Richards' daughter.

According to the news report, Mrs. Richards' daughter and her friends were waiting to cross the street with their bikes. They had stopped to allow the cars to go by. The driver of one of the passing automobiles stopped in the middle of the street and motioned for Andrea and her friends to cross in front of her car. When it was Andrea's turn to cross, the women driving the car pressed on the gas pedal and ran over Andrea. She then placed the car in reverse and backed over Andrea. The driver did this several more times, crushing Andrea's little body. It was reported that the driver and her male passenger were under the influence of drugs when that horrific act was committed.

I never quite understood how or why something so bad could happen to the child of a mother who had reached out to help other kids. Mrs. Richards had blessed us with brand new shoes and left an imprint on my heart through her good deeds and now I was hearing a story about the tragic death of her pride and joy.

Experiencing the loss of so many lives had become difficult for me to comprehend as a young person. The best way for me to deal with the sorrow I felt when viewing the lifeless bodies of my childhood friends, was to imagine how life might have turned out for them, had they chosen a path on "the other side of the fence", so to speak. I could visualize so many of them as successful business men carrying briefcases, with a strong desire to claim the glorious future they were entitled to. Sadly, so many of them had fallen deep into the trap, allowing the darkness to rob them of the promising future they all deserved, but had no way to escape. Well, I knew and accepted that my questions would never be answered because their lives were lost forever, so my imagination and desired dreams for them eventually faded away.

The last body of the childhood friend that I viewed was at a time in my life when my tears had completely dried up. It was during the viewing of Davis' oldest brother Ramone, that my sadness had turned to a form of anger and an enormous amount of ambition to continue striving towards success, for the sake of those whose lives were cut short.

Children born into this huge world should be protected, but unfortunately, many don't get the protection they need and deserve, often leading to feelings of neglect and abandonment for various reasons, which may contribute to many of these children growing up with wounded souls, as they attempt to try and find some sense of identity, meaning and true value in their lives. Many of these children who are left with the responsibility of creating their own distinctive paths in life are also forced to adapt to ways that foster the struggles they encounter, which could very well lead to feelings of lost hope.

In many cases, children who are left with the responsibility of learning to raise themselves, while growing up with little to no protection in their lives are often forced to build their own sense of a protective mechanism, while experiencing so much of the pressure that life has to offer. In addition, they are quite often subjected to the struggle in having to battle through some of the most challenging and difficult times in their mission to survive; an area that I have acquired firsthand knowledge of and experience in. Without the much needed assistance and support offered by others, many of these wounded souls become lost throughout their entire life because they are left without the assistance, support and guidance needed to succeed. While this certainly doesn't stand true for all, it applies to many who desire to escape the traps of bondage, but seem to have no way out.

As a growing child, I always seemed to have a lot of love and care for others and often at times, that same degree of love and care was not reciprocal. Unfortunately, I had to deal with the suffering and pain of having much of my childhood innocence and happiness stripped away by the evil deeds of others, with very few options made available for me to escape the madness. So instead, what seemed to be my only option in my effort to survive, was to build up an invisible wall of protection to shield me throughout my mission to survive so much of the evil and darkness that seemed to surround me wherever I traveled.

In this huge world, there are so many other wounded souls and at the end of the day, those of us who are left with those wounds of life must learn that we have choices. My life most certainly could've gone one of two ways; good or evil, but I chose kindness over evil and happiness over misery.

I have learned throughout the years not to hold onto grudges, anger or guilt. I have chosen to model love and respect for and towards others, which is so much of what our hurting world needs more of.

It is very necessary to maintain some sense of boundaries when dealing with these wounded souls. Many of us may never know how many times we cross the paths of others whose souls have been severely wounded and what degree of pain those individuals have experienced in their lives.

I'll reiterate the fact that the best gift momma left me with was turning her life to Christ, which served to increase my spiritual growth. Growing to understand the beauty of truly living in the light has helped me grasp more of a stronger understanding about my life and survival.

While I may never know or understand why I had to endure so much pain in my lifetime, I do know that I have no regrets because the experiences I was blessed to survive through and overcome molded me into the person I have become today and I am grateful to have chosen kindness over cruelty.

As a culture of society, we must learn to appreciate and respect the lives of others and refrain from mistaking kindness for weakness, which so many in our society tend to do. Many souls are walking this earth and carrying huge burdens of severe pain on their backs from wounds suffered throughout their lifetime.

Throughout the years, I had learned to survive many of life's toughest challenges by fighting back physically, mentally and emotionally. Along my journey of survival, I'd also learned how to suppress so much of the anger and pain that evolved during my mission to overcome those challenges that so frequently clouded my path.

While so much of the embedded pain still exists as a wound in my soul today, I have selected to take the steps necessary to release my pain by sharing my personal story to encourage and inspire others to keep pushing through the storms. It is my prayer and desire to teach my family and other souls to never give up on any dreams, ambitions or desires. Choosing to give up is often a trap and may only serve to set us back from reaching our full potential in life. There is a purpose for all of our lives and in order for us to identify our purpose, we must learn to accept the good with the bad. The secret is, none of us have to settle for the bad, but rather learn how to push through the challenges that appear to threaten our desired future. It is important to understand that many of the challenges we come up against may have very well been placed in our paths for a purpose and in order to understand it, we must develop the strength and belief that the hardships we encounter will improve. Life is only what we choose to make of it through our attitude, beliefs and how we select to live our lives.

While this book may not be for everyone, I have faith that it will reach many, whether young, old, atheists, believers, abusers, victims, children, parents, incarcerated, free and most of all, professionals sharing a desire to go out and assist others; primarily children.

My decision to write and release my book to the public has blessed me with the ability to realize how much pain I was holding onto for so long. The experience has been a true blessing for me in my ability to exercise my freedom through my decision to unveil so much of the darkness that has been trapped inside of me for so long.

Coming from such a dark past of nearly losing my life in many ways, some related to the unhealthy decisions I was making, I have learned to develop a strong desire to instill power, faith and encouragement in others to continue pushing their way out of the darkness and towards the light, no matter how rough and discouraging life may seem. Life is very precious, so we must learn to see the light through whatever circumstances we find ourselves in. There are many situations that we don't always have full control over, which became evident to me after making the decision to surrender my life to Christ.

What I did learn was that "I can do all things through Christ which strengthens me," as quoted in Philippians 4:13 (KJV). I have also learned to accept that many who have lost their lives to the streets along the way had lived the only life they knew best; a life they had grown to become accustomed to.

I recognized, despite being traumatized myself, that I, as a young mom had to do everything possible to save my son from becoming a statistic. All of the lives that were lost had hit too close to home for me and I refused to allow my son, or any other child of mine to get caught up in the web of bondage that I had worked so hard to untangle myself from.

I learned to mentally and emotionally run from the darkness in every effort to save my children. It was no longer about me, but the beautiful children; my angels that I was blessed to be a mom to, as well. I realized life was too short to waste precious time wading around in and sinking into what felt like quicksand. It was my son, my gift from God, who provided me with the motivation to take on risks. He gave me a reason to chase after the success I felt I deserved. CJ was all I had to live for and I knew I would be empty and lost without having him in my life. Everything I was doing as a young mom in my effort to better my life was for CJ's sake and today, that stands true for the rest of my children.

It helped for me to develop healthier ways of perceiving life than what I had experienced in my past. I acquired the ability to step into a new frame of mind that taught me about forgiveness and through my ability to forgive, many of life's battles became so much easier after making the decision to gravitate **Fully Into the Light**.

22

Fully Into the Light

As a child, the value of family was instilled inside of me at a very early age and seemed to have great meaning on both sides. It's just that value of family was lost after my family became succumbed to the darkness. My father made it a priority to pick me up on the weekends and take me around to visit my grandparents, auntie, siblings and cousins on his side of the family. Family was so important to daddy and he did an amazing job in maintaining a special connection with extended relatives, mainly his cousins, which has always been uncommon on momma's side of the family. My relationship with my cousins on momma's side became estranged early on and remains that way to this day.

On momma's side, most of our time spent together as a large family was at my grandfather's rental business. Momma would also take us to family gatherings that were often hosted at one of her brothers homes. Both of momma's brothers happened to reside right across the street from my grandparents, before they each had their homes built from the ground up in rural areas, located in the country. As the night hours set in during many of those family gatherings and the drinking began, the arguing between my mother and her siblings erupted. In the midst of all of the yelling, momma would snatch us up, as she grabbed our belongings to abruptly leave.

On nights that special family occasions ended like that, it would be weeks, sometimes months before momma resumed with speaking to her brothers. Eventually, momma stopped attending the festive holiday gatherings and that's when my relationship with my cousins turned distant. Momma's brothers were very successful Black men and took many of their qualities from my grandfather, which contributed to momma feeling as though she was the "Black sheep" of the family, as she had occasionally relay to us as children.

During those days, the usage of alcohol impacted our family a great deal and that was always the part of the family gathering that I did not like. I never quite understood the reasoning behind all of the arguing that erupted, until I became an adult and realized that the arguing still occurred and it was just momma and us children, leading me to wonder if momma was the antagonist. I do know that my Uncle Duke was certainly not one to bite his tongue when it came to expressing himself.

By that time of my adulthood momma had completely recovered from her addiction to alcohol, but the emotional scars and pain still resided within her, something I had learned about after completing many of the therapeutic courses I was required to take while studying for my undergraduate degree in Human Services. I had learned that holidays can be especially difficult for many who have suffered great losses and experienced a lot of trauma and pain in their lives and unfortunately, my mother fell into this category.

The experience of all of the yelling and arguing that occurred during the holidays certainly left me with a bad image of family festivities and togetherness, but I fought for the chance to prevent subjecting my own family to many of the same struggles.

Considering the fact that momma lost her mother to alcoholism at age 13 and later, her only sister, who had accepted the responsibility as a second mom to my mother, I realized that momma's sorrow ran deep. These times were very crucial times in momma's life and really should have been more meaningful experiences for momma, where fond memories were created.

Momma was a lonely soul inside who trusted very few people in her lifetime. There were times I felt like momma didn't even trust me and it was all due to feelings of betrayal and abandonment that so heavily wore her down throughout her lifetime.

I have always desired for the holidays and special occasions to have meaning for my own immediate family and therefore, felt it necessary to create strong memories that my own family will hopefully cherish forever.

While there are no perfect families, we all have the ability to strive to create the best memories possible, especially when children are involved.

Through my studies, as well as my own personal experiences and struggles throughout my early childhood and teenage years, I've learned that the chances are far greater for a child, or children of alcoholics to repeat the vicious cycle of becoming alcoholics themselves and I refused to repeat a cycle that I knew would alter my mind and behavior in the presence of my family. I also refused to allow myself to become stripped of the person I was created to be.

After the loss of both of my parents, I encountered a phase in my life of completely alienating myself from many loved ones, feeling as though I had no extended family and I would often express sadness to my husband and children about feeling so alone. My brother Jeris was all I had from my extended family. My sister, Shereese and I have never really experienced a truly genuine, loving and close sibling relationship with one another and I've accepted the fact that no matter how much one desires change, if the effort is not reciprocal, then that desire for change unfortunately may never occur.

With regard to my father's side of the family, I never really felt that I belonged since those were the words frequently relayed to me by momma. It was always just my father who I was closest to. Even though daddy tried so hard to keep me engaged with my family members, even to the point of sending me to Washington D.C. to spend a portion of the summer with my cousins, everything seemed to fade after his passing.

Daddy was the glue in the family who strived to keep everyone unified and when I lost daddy, everything seemed to fall apart for me in relation to maintaining a connection. I had lost connection with so many that I once shared a family bond with and that was a long period of a very lonely life for me.

Now, as a parent, I have managed to hold on strong to my own children and have worked hard to teach them the true value of family.

In realizing I was repeating the same unhealthy cycle and lifestyle in isolating myself and my immediate family from other family members, I knew I needed to make changes for the sake of my children, to prevent them from growing up and turning their backs on loved ones. Sometimes, the strive in maintaining a strong family bond may not always work out for the best and that is okay.

I am constantly teaching and encouraging togetherness to my children and hope that they are blessed with the ability to continue building a strong and healthy family bond in an effort to keep the chains of bondage broken.

I recently had the pleasure of reuniting with family members on my father's side and the experience has been wonderful for me. I have also been blessed to maintain a relationship with Uncle Darren who happens to be my only living uncle on momma's side of the family and one who has always inspired me. In addition, I have developed a close relationship with my sister, Frieda and her family through marriage on Shereese's father's side, who have all managed to embrace me and my family with open arms. Through their strong effort, my life, as well as the life of my husband and children, have completely been touched.

My relationship with Benny has also remained strong throughout the years with the help and continued support from Desmond. We've been invited to holiday festivities and during those times we were able to attend, many fond memories were created.

I have found nothing but great pride stemming from both sides of my family and feel completely proud in knowing that there are true family members out there who will always share a genuine love for me and my family.

To my entire family, stemming from my father's, mother's, husband's and Benny's side, and also to all of my friends who have remained true throughout the years, I love all of you with a passion and sincerely thank you for all of the love and support each and every one of you have shown to me and my family. It is because of you all that my world has become a better and much healthier place.

ABOUT THE AUTHOR

Dionne is a native of Colorado, born and raised in the City of Denver. Dionne is a wife; mother of five and lifetime mentor. The Shadows of Darkness: Then Came the Light is Dionne's first Memoir. Growing up in the City of Denver and losing many childhood friends to what is known as the Summer of Violence, Dionne decided to make a difference with her life by stepping out on faith to accomplish goals that once appeared impossible to attain. Through her strength and courage, Dionne vowed to 'Fight in the ring of life' for what she desired in her heart and now striving to give back to other children who may struggle with seeing a clear path out.

To contact Dionne, please visit her website at
www.dionnewilliamsvoss.com